Contents

About Literacy Centers
Grades 2–3

What's Great About This Book

Centers are a wonderful, fun way for students to practice important skills. The 14 centers in this book are self-contained and portable. Students may work at a desk or even on the floor. Once you've made the centers, they're ready to use at any time.

What's in This Book

Teacher direction page
includes a description of the student task

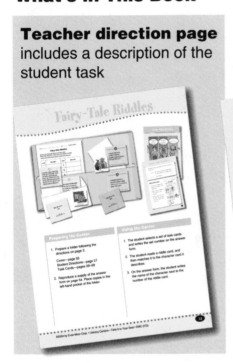

Full-color materials
needed for the center

Reproducible answer forms

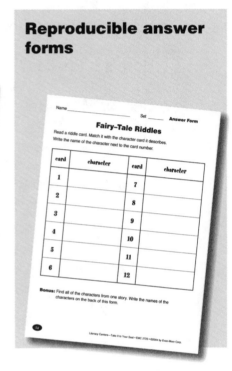

How to Use the Centers

The centers are intended for skill practice, not to introduce skills. It is important to model the use of each center before students do the task independently.

Questions to Consider:

- Will students select a center, or will you assign the centers?
- Will there be a specific block of time for centers, or will the centers be used throughout the day?
- Where will you place the centers for easy access by students?
- What procedure will students use when they need help with the center tasks?
- Where will students store completed work?
- How will you track the tasks and centers completed by each student?

Making a File Folder Center

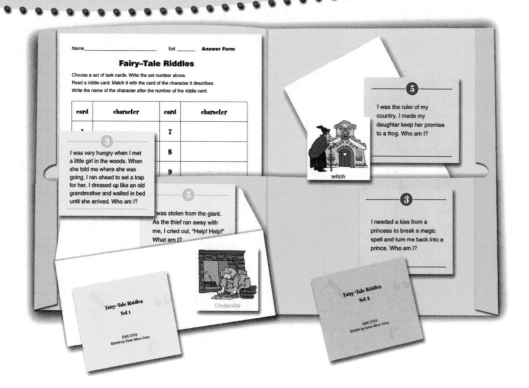

Materials

- folder with pockets
- envelopes or plastic self-locking bags
- marking pens and pencils
- scissors
- two-sided tape

Folder cover

Folder back cover
Student Direction page

Steps to Follow

1. Laminate the cover. Tape it to the front of the folder.

2. Laminate the student direction page. Tape it to the back of the folder.

3. Place answer forms, writing paper, and any other supplies in the left-hand pocket.

4. Laminate the task cards. Place each set of cards in a labeled envelope or plastic self-locking bag. Place the envelopes and sorting mat (if required for the center) in the right-hand pocket.

Folder centers are easily stored in a box or file crate. Students take a folder to their desks to complete the task.

Center Checklist

Student Names

Centers

Super Sentence Sort												
How Is It Spelled?												
Real or Make-Believe?												
Alphabetical Order												
Fairy-Tale Riddles												
Draw and Write												
Antonyms												
Synonyms												
As Busy as a Bee!												
Top Ten												
It's in the Mail												
They Sound the Same												
More Than One												
More Than One Meaning												

Literacy Centers—Take It to Your Seat • EMC 2723 • ©2004 by Evan-Moor Corp.

Super Sentence Sort

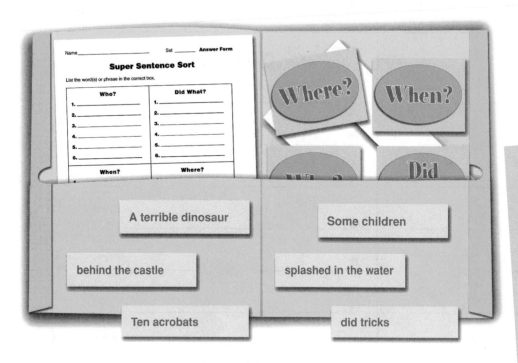

Preparing the Center

1. Prepare a folder following the directions on page 3.

   Cover—page 7
   Student Directions—page 9
   Sorting Cards—page 11
   Task Cards—pages 13 and 15

2. Reproduce a supply of the answer form on page 6. Place copies in the left-hand pocket of the folder.

Using the Center

1. The student takes an answer form and all the cards.

2. The student lays out the sorting cards **Who? Did What? Where? When?**, and then places the task cards in the correct category.

3. The student lists each word(s) or phrase in the correct box on the answer form.

4. Next, the student selects one card from each category and uses the words to write a complete super sentence.

Super Sentence Sort

List each word or phrase in the correct box.

Who?	**Did What?**
1. _____	1. _____
2. _____	2. _____
3. _____	3. _____
4. _____	4. _____
5. _____	5. _____
6. _____	6. _____
When?	**Where?**
1. _____	1. _____
2. _____	2. _____
3. _____	3. _____
4. _____	4. _____
5. _____	5. _____
6. _____	6. _____

Take one card from each box. Write a super sentence.

_____

_____

Bonus: Choose four new cards and write more super sentences on the back
of this form.

Super Sentence Sort

Super Sentence Sort

A **sentence** is one or more words that express a complete thought.

A **super sentence** contains descriptive words and phrases that tell where and when.

Some children hid.

Some children hid under a log all afternoon.

Follow these steps:

1. Take all of the cards and an answer form.

2. Lay out the question cards **Who? Did What? Where? When?** Read the word and phrase cards and place them in the correct category.

3. List the words and phrases on the answer form.

4. Take one card from each category and write a super sentence.

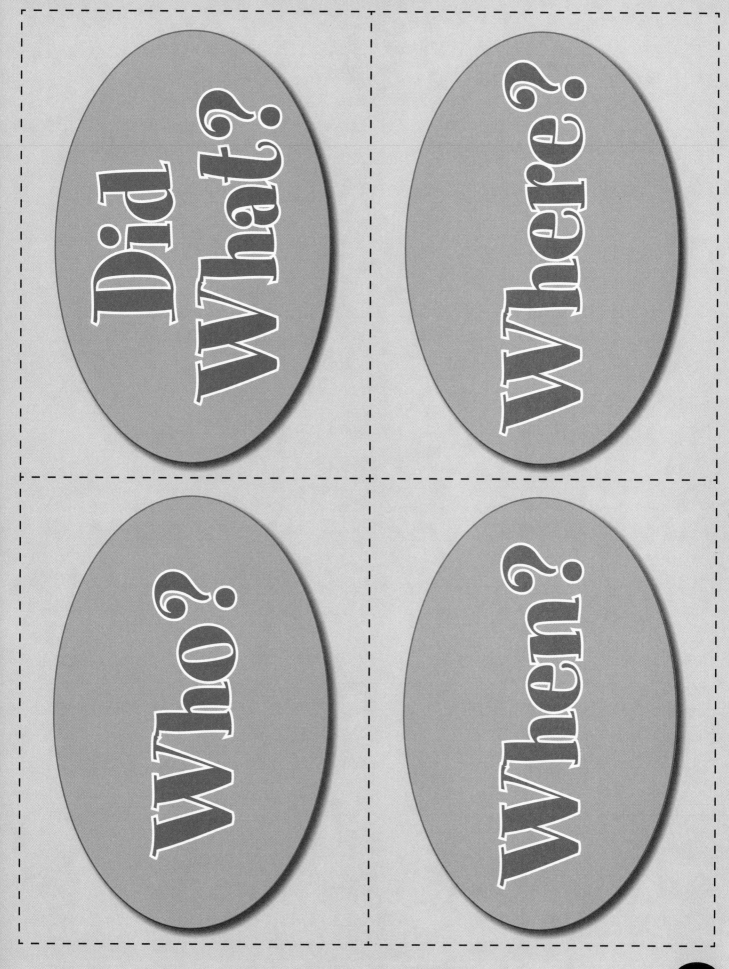

Super Sentence Sort
EMC 2723
©2004 by Evan-Moor Corp.

Super Sentence Sort
EMC 2723
©2004 by Evan-Moor Corp.

Super Sentence Sort
EMC 2723
©2004 by Evan-Moor Corp.

Super Sentence Sort
EMC 2723
©2004 by Evan-Moor Corp.

nibbled fruit

vanished

splashed in the water

hid

fell asleep

did tricks

Some children

My pet dog

A green parrot

A terrible dinosaur

That lazy giant

Ten acrobats

Super Sentence Sort
EMC 2723
©2004 by Evan-Moor Corp.

Super Sentence Sort
EMC 2723
©2004 by Evan-Moor Corp.

Super Sentence Sort
EMC 2723
©2004 by Evan-Moor Corp.

Super Sentence Sort
EMC 2723
©2004 by Evan-Moor Corp.

Super Sentence Sort
EMC 2723
©2004 by Evan-Moor Corp.

Super Sentence Sort
EMC 2723
©2004 by Evan-Moor Corp.

Super Sentence Sort
EMC 2723
©2004 by Evan-Moor Corp.

Super Sentence Sort
EMC 2723
©2004 by Evan-Moor Corp.

Super Sentence Sort
EMC 2723
©2004 by Evan-Moor Corp.

Super Sentence Sort
EMC 2723
©2004 by Evan-Moor Corp.

Super Sentence Sort
EMC 2723
©2004 by Evan-Moor Corp.

Super Sentence Sort
EMC 2723
©2004 by Evan-Moor Corp.

in a dark cave

under an old log

behind the castle

long ago

at 6:00

for many days

in the treetops

in the backyard

in a circus tent

a moment ago

all afternoon

late one night

Super Sentence Sort
EMC 2723
©2004 by Evan-Moor Corp.

Super Sentence Sort
EMC 2723
©2004 by Evan-Moor Corp.

Super Sentence Sort
EMC 2723
©2004 by Evan-Moor Corp.

Super Sentence Sort
EMC 2723
©2004 by Evan-Moor Corp.

Super Sentence Sort
EMC 2723
©2004 by Evan-Moor Corp.

Super Sentence Sort
EMC 2723
©2004 by Evan-Moor Corp.

Super Sentence Sort
EMC 2723
©2004 by Evan-Moor Corp.

Super Sentence Sort
EMC 2723
©2004 by Evan-Moor Corp.

Super Sentence Sort
EMC 2723
©2004 by Evan-Moor Corp.

Super Sentence Sort
EMC 2723
©2004 by Evan-Moor Corp.

Super Sentence Sort
EMC 2723
©2004 by Evan-Moor Corp.

Super Sentence Sort
EMC 2723
©2004 by Evan-Moor Corp.

How Is It Spelled?

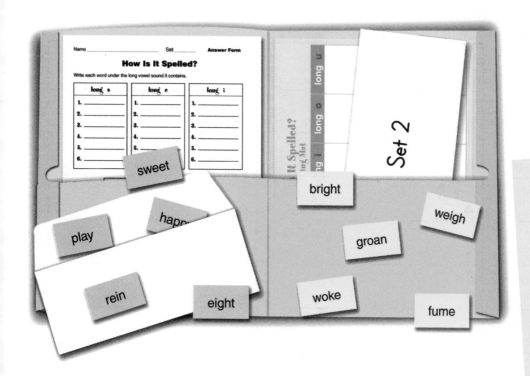

Preparing the Center

1. Prepare a folder following the directions on page 3.

   Cover—page 19
   Student Directions—page 21
   Sorting Mat—page 23
   Task Cards—pages 25 and 27

2. Reproduce a supply of the answer form on page 18. Place copies in the left-hand pocket of the folder.

Using the Center

1. The student chooses a set of task cards and writes the set number on the answer form.

2. Using the sorting mat, the student places each word card under the correct long vowel sound.

3. The student writes each word under its vowel sound on the answer form.

How Is It Spelled?

Write each word under the long vowel sound it contains.

long a
1. _____
2. _____
3. _____
4. _____
5. _____
6. _____

long e
1. _____
2. _____
3. _____
4. _____
5. _____
6. _____

long i
1. _____
2. _____
3. _____
4. _____
5. _____
6. _____

long o
1. _____
2. _____
3. _____
4. _____
5. _____
6. _____

long u
1. _____
2. _____
3. _____
4. _____
5. _____
6. _____

Bonus: Circle the letter or letters in each word that spell the long vowel sound.

Literacy Centers—Take It to Your Seat • EMC 2723 • ©2004 by Evan-Moor Corp.

How Is It Spelled?

A long vowel sound may have several different spellings. For example:

long a — play, train

long e — be, see

long i — night, tie

long o — boat, toe

long u — cute, menu

Follow these steps:

1. Choose a set of cards and write the set number on the answer form. Take the sorting mat.

2. Read each word card and place it under the long vowel sound it contains.

3. Write each word under its long vowel sound on the answer form.

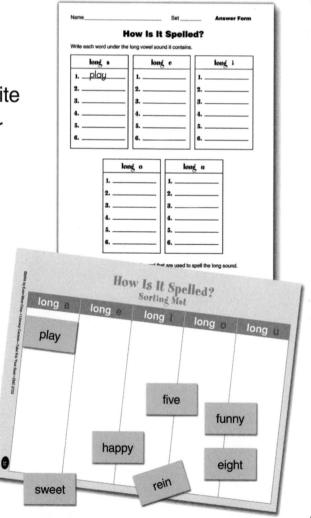

How Is It Spelled?
Sorting Mat

long a	long e	long i	long o	long u

How Is It Spelled?

©2004 by Evan-Moor Corp

EMC 2723

play	train	eight	rein
April	me	happy	sweet
eat	funny	bead	pie
I	cry	five	take
light	my	go	throw
toe	joke	float	those
cute	human	menu	uniform
cube	bugle		

How Is It Spelled?
Set 1

EMC 2723
©2004 by Evan-Moor Corp.

How Is It Spelled?
Set 1

EMC 2723
©2004 by Evan-Moor Corp.

How Is It Spelled?
Set 1

EMC 2723
©2004 by Evan-Moor Corp.

How Is It Spelled?
Set 1

EMC 2723
©2004 by Evan-Moor Corp.

How Is It Spelled?
Set 1

EMC 2723
©2004 by Evan-Moor Corp.

How Is It Spelled?
Set 1

EMC 2723
©2004 by Evan-Moor Corp.

How Is It Spelled?
Set 1

EMC 2723
©2004 by Evan-Moor Corp.

How Is It Spelled?
Set 1

EMC 2723
©2004 by Evan-Moor Corp.

How Is It Spelled?
Set 1

EMC 2723
©2004 by Evan-Moor Corp.

How Is It Spelled?
Set 1

EMC 2723
©2004 by Evan-Moor Corp.

How Is It Spelled?
Set 1

EMC 2723
©2004 by Evan-Moor Corp.

How Is It Spelled?
Set 1

EMC 2723
©2004 by Evan-Moor Corp.

How Is It Spelled?
Set 1

EMC 2723
©2004 by Evan-Moor Corp.

How Is It Spelled?
Set 1

EMC 2723
©2004 by Evan-Moor Corp.

How Is It Spelled?
Set 1

EMC 2723
©2004 by Evan-Moor Corp.

How Is It Spelled?
Set 1

EMC 2723
©2004 by Evan-Moor Corp.

How Is It Spelled?
Set 1

EMC 2723
©2004 by Evan-Moor Corp.

How Is It Spelled?
Set 1

EMC 2723
©2004 by Evan-Moor Corp.

How Is It Spelled?
Set 1

EMC 2723
©2004 by Evan-Moor Corp.

How Is It Spelled?
Set 1

EMC 2723
©2004 by Evan-Moor Corp.

How Is It Spelled?
Set 1

EMC 2723
©2004 by Evan-Moor Corp.

How Is It Spelled?
Set 1

EMC 2723
©2004 by Evan-Moor Corp.

How Is It Spelled?
Set 1

EMC 2723
©2004 by Evan-Moor Corp.

How Is It Spelled?
Set 1

EMC 2723
©2004 by Evan-Moor Corp.

How Is It Spelled?
Set 1

EMC 2723
©2004 by Evan-Moor Corp.

How Is It Spelled?
Set 1

EMC 2723
©2004 by Evan-Moor Corp.

How Is It Spelled?
Set 1

EMC 2723
©2004 by Evan-Moor Corp.

How Is It Spelled?
Set 1

EMC 2723
©2004 by Evan-Moor Corp.

How Is It Spelled?
Set 1

EMC 2723
©2004 by Evan-Moor Corp.

How Is It Spelled?
Set 1

EMC 2723
©2004 by Evan-Moor Corp.

weigh	face	faint	spray
they	nail	tribe	fire
bright	tie	eye	fry
beam	flute	bumpy	many
tweed	grease	bleach	hose
loan	groan	hoe	phone
woke	mule	cue	fuse
truth	fume		

How Is It Spelled?
Set 2

EMC 2723
©2004 by Evan-Moor Corp.

How Is It Spelled?
Set 2

EMC 2723
©2004 by Evan-Moor Corp.

How Is It Spelled?
Set 2

EMC 2723
©2004 by Evan-Moor Corp.

How Is It Spelled?
Set 2

EMC 2723
©2004 by Evan-Moor Corp.

How Is It Spelled?
Set 2

EMC 2723
©2004 by Evan-Moor Corp.

How Is It Spelled?
Set 2

EMC 2723
©2004 by Evan-Moor Corp.

How Is It Spelled?
Set 2

EMC 2723
©2004 by Evan-Moor Corp.

How Is It Spelled?
Set 2

EMC 2723
©2004 by Evan-Moor Corp.

How Is It Spelled?
Set 2

EMC 2723
©2004 by Evan-Moor Corp.

How Is It Spelled?
Set 2

EMC 2723
©2004 by Evan-Moor Corp.

How Is It Spelled?
Set 2

EMC 2723
©2004 by Evan-Moor Corp.

How Is It Spelled?
Set 2

EMC 2723
©2004 by Evan-Moor Corp.

How Is It Spelled?
Set 2

EMC 2723
©2004 by Evan-Moor Corp.

How Is It Spelled?
Set 2

EMC 2723
©2004 by Evan-Moor Corp.

How Is It Spelled?
Set 2

EMC 2723
©2004 by Evan-Moor Corp.

How Is It Spelled?
Set 2

EMC 2723
©2004 by Evan-Moor Corp.

How Is It Spelled?
Set 2

EMC 2723
©2004 by Evan-Moor Corp.

How Is It Spelled?
Set 2

EMC 2723
©2004 by Evan-Moor Corp.

How Is It Spelled?
Set 2

EMC 2723
©2004 by Evan-Moor Corp.

How Is It Spelled?
Set 2

EMC 2723
©2004 by Evan-Moor Corp.

How Is It Spelled?
Set 2

EMC 2723
©2004 by Evan-Moor Corp.

How Is It Spelled?
Set 2

EMC 2723
©2004 by Evan-Moor Corp.

How Is It Spelled?
Set 2

EMC 2723
©2004 by Evan-Moor Corp.

How Is It Spelled?
Set 2

EMC 2723
©2004 by Evan-Moor Corp.

How Is It Spelled?
Set 2

EMC 2723
©2004 by Evan-Moor Corp.

How Is It Spelled?
Set 2

EMC 2723
©2004 by Evan-Moor Corp.

How Is It Spelled?
Set 2

EMC 2723
©2004 by Evan-Moor Corp.

How Is It Spelled?
Set 2

EMC 2723
©2004 by Evan-Moor Corp.

How Is It Spelled?
Set 2

EMC 2723
©2004 by Evan-Moor Corp.

How Is It Spelled?
Set 2

EMC 2723
©2004 by Evan-Moor Corp.

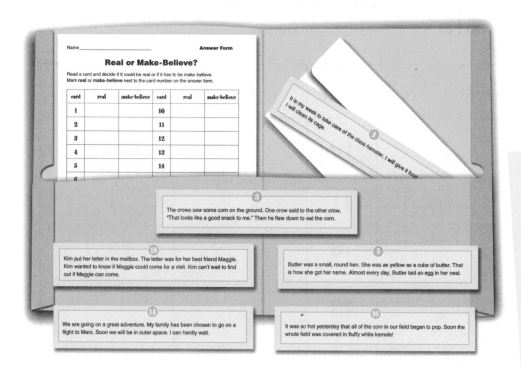

Preparing the Center

1. Prepare a folder following the directions on page 3.

   Cover—page 31
   Student Directions—page 33
   Task Cards—pages 35–39

2. Reproduce a supply of the answer form on page 30. Place copies in the left-hand pocket of the folder.

Using the Center

1. The student takes the cards and an answer form.

2. The student reads each sentence card and decides if the sentence describes something that is real or something that is make-believe.

3. On the answer form, the student marks **real** or **make-believe** next to each sentence number.

Real or Make-Believe?

Read a card and decide if it could be real or if it has to be make-believe.
Mark **real** or **make-believe** next to the card number below.

card	real	make-believe	card	real	make-believe
1			10		
2			11		
3			12		
4			13		
5			14		
6			15		
7			16		
8			17		
9			18		

Bonus: Think of one thing that you know is real. Write it below.
　　　　　 Think of one thing that you know is make-believe. Write it below.

Real: _____

Make-believe: _____

Real or Make-Believe?

Some stories are **real**. They are about things that could really happen. Other stories are **make-believe**. They are about things that could not happen.

real: The slow green turtle made its way through the tall grass.

make-believe: The large purple turtle skipped all the way to the soda shop.

Follow these steps:

1. Take the sentence cards and an answer form.

2. Read a card and decide if it could be real or if it is make-believe.

3. Mark **real** or **make-believe** next to the sentence number on the answer form.

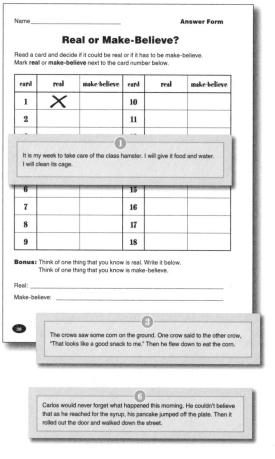

Name_____   Answer Form

Real or Make-Believe?

Read a card and decide if it could be real or if it has to be make-believe.
Mark **real** or **make-believe** next to the card number below.

card	real	make-believe	card	real	make-believe
1	X		10		
2			11		
6			15		
7			16		
8			17		
9			18		

① It is my week to take care of the class hamster. I will give it food and water. I will clean its cage.

Bonus: Think of one thing that you know is real. Write it below.
Think of one thing that you know is make-believe.

Real: _____

Make-believe: _____

30

③ The crows saw some corn on the ground. One crow said to the other crow, "That looks like a good snack to me." Then he flew down to eat the corn.

⑤ Butter was a small, round hen. She was as yellow as a cube of butter. That is how she got her name. Almost every day, Butter laid an egg in her nest.

② The gorilla put on his hat and went out the door. He walked down the street. Soon, he was at the ice-cream shop. In he went to buy an ice-cream cone.

⑥ Carlos would never forget what happened this morning. He couldn't believe that as he reached for the syrup, his pancake jumped off the plate. Then it rolled out the door and walked down the street.

1

It is my week to take care of the class hamster. I will give it food and water. I will clean its cage.

2

The gorilla put on his hat and went out the door. He walked down the street. Soon, he was at the ice-cream shop. In he went to buy an ice-cream cone.

3

The crows saw some corn on the ground. One crow said to the other crow, "That looks like a good snack to me." Then he flew down to eat the corn.

4

Drip, drop. Drip, drop. Rain came falling down from the sky. Soon, there were puddles everywhere.

5

Butter was a small, round hen. She was as yellow as a cube of butter. That is how she got her name. Almost every day, Butter laid an egg in her nest.

6

Carlos would never forget what happened this morning. He couldn't believe that as he reached for the syrup, his pancake jumped off the plate. Then it rolled out the door and walked down the street.

Real or Make-Believe?

EMC 2723
©2004 by Evan-Moor Corp.

Real or Make-Believe?

EMC 2723
©2004 by Evan-Moor Corp.

Real or Make-Believe?

EMC 2723
©2004 by Evan-Moor Corp.

Real or Make-Believe?

EMC 2723
©2004 by Evan-Moor Corp.

Real or Make-Believe?

EMC 2723
©2004 by Evan-Moor Corp.

Real or Make-Believe?

EMC 2723
©2004 by Evan-Moor Corp.

7

Sam saw bees buzzing around the flowers. The busy bees were collecting nectar to take back to their hive. "The bees will use the nectar to make honey," thought Sam.

8

It has been snowing for a long time. First, the snowflakes were white and fluffy. Then, pink snowflakes began to fall. Next, green snowflakes fell. Soon, snowflakes all the colors of the rainbow were falling. What a great snowstorm!

9

When I get hungry, I just get out my blue and white tablecloth. I spread the cloth on a table and say, "Cloth, feed me." Soon, the table is covered with good food to eat.

10

A little gray mouse lives in the wall of my kitchen. The mouse only comes out when I am gone. The mouse looks for food to nibble. If I come back, the mouse hides in its hole.

11

Pete went to the garden to dig up a carrot. He pulled and pulled and pulled. "Why won't this carrot come out?" said Pete. All of a sudden, a huge carrot popped out of the dirt. The carrot was taller than Pete. It was 10 feet tall!

12

Bats have wings and they can fly, but they are not birds. They are mammals. Bat wings are covered in skin. Bird wings are covered with feathers.

Real or Make-Believe?

Real or Make-Believe?

Real or Make-Believe?

Real or Make-Believe?

Real or Make-Believe?

Real or Make-Believe?

13

The farmer found a white goose swimming in the pond on his farm. He took the goose home and put it in a pen. The next morning, the farmer found a golden egg in the pen. "How lucky I am," he thought.

14

We are going on a great adventure. My family has been chosen to go on a flight to Mars. Soon, we will be in outer space. I can hardly wait!

15

One morning, Mary saw blackbirds eating the corn in her cornfield. She grabbed a metal dishpan and a big spoon. Out she ran into the cornfield. She banged on the dishpan with the spoon. What a racket she made! Soon, all the blackbirds were gone!

16

It was so hot yesterday that all of the corn in our field began to pop. Soon, the whole field was covered in fluffy white kernels!

17

What is black and white and looks like a big bear? A giant panda! There are very few giant pandas left in the world. In the wild, they live in bamboo forests. These forests are found only in parts of China.

18

Kim put her letter in the mailbox. The letter was for her best friend Maggie. Kim wanted to know if Maggie could come for a visit. Kim can't wait to find out if Maggie can come.

Real or Make-Believe?

EMC 2723
©2004 by Evan-Moor Corp.

Real or Make-Believe?

EMC 2723
©2004 by Evan-Moor Corp.

Real or Make-Believe?

EMC 2723
©2004 by Evan-Moor Corp.

Real or Make-Believe?

EMC 2723
©2004 by Evan-Moor Corp.

Real or Make-Believe?

EMC 2723
©2004 by Evan-Moor Corp.

Real or Make-Believe?

EMC 2723
©2004 by Evan-Moor Corp.

Alphabetical Order

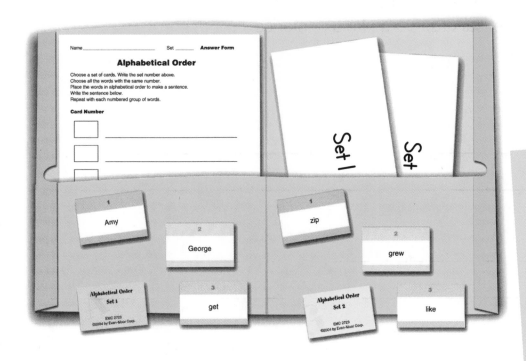
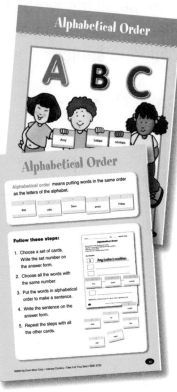

Preparing the Center

1. Prepare a folder following the directions on page 3.

   Cover—page 43
   Student Directions—page 45
   Task Cards—pages 47–51

2. Reproduce a supply of the answer form on page 42. Place copies in the left-hand pocket of the folder.

Using the Center

1. The student chooses a set of task cards and writes the set number on the answer form.

2. The student selects all the cards with the same number and places the words in alphabetical order to form a sentence.

3. The student writes the sentence beside the correct number on the answer form.

Alphabetical Order

Choose all the words with the same number.
Place the words in alphabetical order to make a sentence.
Write the sentence below.

Card Number

Bonus: Write a sentence of your own with the words in alphabetical order.

Literacy Centers—Take It to Your Seat • EMC 2723 • ©2004 by Evan-Moor Corp.

A B C

Amy   baked   cookies

Alphabetical Order

Alphabetical order means putting words in the same order as the letters of the alphabet.

1	1	1	1	1
Bob	calls	Darci	every	Friday

Follow these steps:

1. Choose a set of cards. Write the set number on the answer form.

2. Choose all the words with the same number.

3. Put the words in alphabetical order to make a sentence.

4. Write the sentence on the answer form.

5. Repeat the steps with all the other cards.

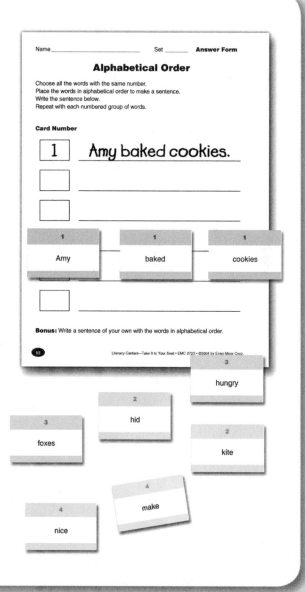

1	1	1
Amy	baked	cookies

2	2	2
George	hid	Jake's

2	3	3
kite	Even	foxes

3	3	4
get	hungry	Lilies

4	4	4
make	nice	outdoor

4	5	5
plants	Kim	likes

5	5	5
making	noise	outside

6	6	6
Claire	drew	eight

6	6	1
fancy	goldfish	My

1	1	1
parka	won't	zip

2	2	2
Bobby	grew	orange

2	3	3
yams	I	like

Alphabetical Order **Set 1** EMC 2723 ©2004 by Evan-Moor Corp.	**Alphabetical Order** **Set 1** EMC 2723 ©2004 by Evan-Moor Corp.	**Alphabetical Order** **Set 1** EMC 2723 ©2004 by Evan-Moor Corp.
Alphabetical Order **Set 1** EMC 2723 ©2004 by Evan-Moor Corp.	**Alphabetical Order** **Set 1** EMC 2723 ©2004 by Evan-Moor Corp.	**Alphabetical Order** **Set 1** EMC 2723 ©2004 by Evan-Moor Corp.
Alphabetical Order **Set 2** EMC 2723 ©2004 by Evan-Moor Corp.	**Alphabetical Order** **Set 1** EMC 2723 ©2004 by Evan-Moor Corp.	**Alphabetical Order** **Set 1** EMC 2723 ©2004 by Evan-Moor Corp.
Alphabetical Order **Set 2** EMC 2723 ©2004 by Evan-Moor Corp.	**Alphabetical Order** **Set 2** EMC 2723 ©2004 by Evan-Moor Corp.	**Alphabetical Order** **Set 2** EMC 2723 ©2004 by Evan-Moor Corp.
Alphabetical Order **Set 2** EMC 2723 ©2004 by Evan-Moor Corp.	**Alphabetical Order** **Set 2** EMC 2723 ©2004 by Evan-Moor Corp.	**Alphabetical Order** **Set 2** EMC 2723 ©2004 by Evan-Moor Corp.
Alphabetical Order **Set 2** EMC 2723 ©2004 by Evan-Moor Corp.	**Alphabetical Order** **Set 2** EMC 2723 ©2004 by Evan-Moor Corp.	**Alphabetical Order** **Set 2** EMC 2723 ©2004 by Evan-Moor Corp.

3	3	3
playing	the	xylophone

4	4	4
Don	feeds	giraffes

4	4	4
in	the	zoo

5	5	5
Sam	squirted	Susan's

5	6	6
sweater	When	will

6	6	6
William	wrestle	Wyatt

Alphabetical Order

Set 2

EMC 2723
©2004 by Evan-Moor Corp.

Alphabetical Order

Set 2

EMC 2723
©2004 by Evan-Moor Corp.

Alphabetical Order

Set 2

EMC 2723
©2004 by Evan-Moor Corp.

Alphabetical Order

Set 2

EMC 2723
©2004 by Evan-Moor Corp.

Alphabetical Order

Set 2

EMC 2723
©2004 by Evan-Moor Corp.

Alphabetical Order

Set 2

EMC 2723
©2004 by Evan-Moor Corp.

Alphabetical Order

Set 2

EMC 2723
©2004 by Evan-Moor Corp.

Alphabetical Order

Set 2

EMC 2723
©2004 by Evan-Moor Corp.

Alphabetical Order

Set 2

EMC 2723
©2004 by Evan-Moor Corp.

Alphabetical Order

Set 2

EMC 2723
©2004 by Evan-Moor Corp.

Alphabetical Order

Set 2

EMC 2723
©2004 by Evan-Moor Corp.

Alphabetical Order

Set 2

EMC 2723
©2004 by Evan-Moor Corp.

Alphabetical Order

Set 2

EMC 2723
©2004 by Evan-Moor Corp.

Alphabetical Order

Set 2

EMC 2723
©2004 by Evan-Moor Corp.

Alphabetical Order

Set 2

EMC 2723
©2004 by Evan-Moor Corp.

Alphabetical Order

Set 2

EMC 2723
©2004 by Evan-Moor Corp.

Alphabetical Order

Set 2

EMC 2723
©2004 by Evan-Moor Corp.

Alphabetical Order

Set 2

EMC 2723
©2004 by Evan-Moor Corp.

Fairy-Tale Riddles

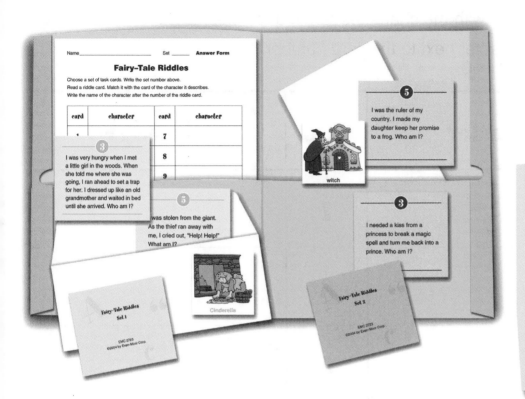

Preparing the Center

1. Prepare a folder following the directions on page 3.

   Cover—page 55
   Student Directions—page 57
   Task Cards—pages 59–69

2. Reproduce a supply of the answer form on page 54. Place copies in the left-hand pocket of the folder.

Using the Center

1. The student selects a set of task cards and writes the set number on the answer form.

2. The student reads a riddle card, and then matches it to the character card it describes.

3. On the answer form, the student writes the name of the character next to the number of the riddle card.

Fairy–Tale Riddles

Read a riddle card. Match it with the character card it describes.

Write the name of the character next to the card number.

card	character	card	character
1		7	
2		8	
3		9	
4		10	
5		11	
6		12	

Bonus: Find all of the characters from one story. Write the names of the characters on the back of this form.

Literacy Centers—Take It to Your Seat • EMC 2723 • ©2004 by Evan-Moor Corp.

Fairy-Tale Riddles

Fairy-Tale Riddles

A puzzling question or problem to be solved or guessed is called a **riddle**.

riddle: We are nursery rhyme mice that cannot see. There are three of us. Who are we?

answer: Three blind mice

Follow these steps:

1. Choose a set of task cards. Write the set number on the answer form.

2. Read a riddle card. Match it to the character card it describes.

3. On the answer form, write the name of the character next to the number of the riddle card.

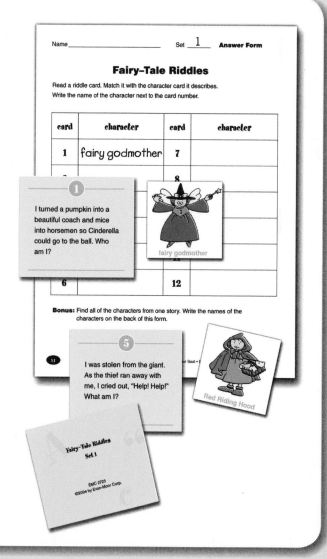

1

I turned a pumpkin into a beautiful coach and mice into horsemen so Cinderella could go to the ball. Who am I?

2

I lived in a castle in the clouds. A boy stole my bag of gold, my magic hen, and my singing harp. Who am I?

3

I was very hungry when I met a little girl in the woods. When she told me where she was going, I ran ahead to set a trap for her. I dressed up like an old grandmother and waited in bed until she arrived. Who am I?

4

An acorn landed on my head. I thought the sky was falling. Who am I?

5

I was stolen from the giant. As the thief ran away with me, I cried out, "Help! Help!" What am I?

6

I met a beautiful girl at my ball. She ran away at midnight. All I had left was her glass slipper. Who am I?

Fairy-Tale Riddles

Set 1

EMC 2723
©2004 by Evan-Moor Corp.

Fairy-Tale Riddles

Set 1

EMC 2723
©2004 by Evan-Moor Corp.

Fairy-Tale Riddles

Set 1

EMC 2723
©2004 by Evan-Moor Corp.

Fairy-Tale Riddles

Set 1

EMC 2723
©2004 by Evan-Moor Corp.

Fairy-Tale Riddles

Set 1

EMC 2723
©2004 by Evan-Moor Corp.

Fairy-Tale Riddles

Set 1

EMC 2723
©2004 by Evan-Moor Corp.

7

A frightened hen ran up to me and said, "The sky is falling!" Who am I?

8

I was working in the woods when I heard a little girl scream. I ran to help her. A wolf was chasing her around the house. I rescued the little girl. Who am I?

9

I saw a group of farm animals running around. They thought the sky was falling. I led the silly animals into my cave. Who am I?

10

I climbed up a gigantic beanpole that reached into the clouds. I went into the giant's castle and took his gold and his magic hen and harp. Who am I?

11

My wicked stepmother made me do all of the hard work. My fairy godmother sent me to the ball to meet the prince. At midnight, my beautiful gown turned back into rags. Who am I?

12

My grandmother was sick. Mother sent me to Grandmother's house with a basket of good things for her to eat. Who am I?

Fairy-Tale Riddles
Set 1

EMC 2723
©2004 by Evan-Moor Corp.

Fairy-Tale Riddles
Set 1

EMC 2723
©2004 by Evan-Moor Corp.

Fairy-Tale Riddles
Set 1

EMC 2723
©2004 by Evan-Moor Corp.

Fairy-Tale Riddles
Set 1

EMC 2723
©2004 by Evan-Moor Corp.

Fairy-Tale Riddles
Set 1

EMC 2723
©2004 by Evan-Moor Corp.

Fairy-Tale Riddles
Set 1

EMC 2723
©2004 by Evan-Moor Corp.

giant

wolf

Cinderella

harp

prince

woodsman

fairy godmother

Jack

Red Riding Hood

Henny Penny

Turkey Lurkey

Foxy Loxy

Fairy-Tale Riddles

Set 1

EMC 2723
©2004 by Evan-Moor Corp.

Fairy-Tale Riddles

Set 1

EMC 2723
©2004 by Evan-Moor Corp.

Fairy-Tale Riddles

Set 1

EMC 2723
©2004 by Evan-Moor Corp.

Fairy-Tale Riddles

Set 1

EMC 2723
©2004 by Evan-Moor Corp.

Fairy-Tale Riddles

Set 1

EMC 2723
©2004 by Evan-Moor Corp.

Fairy-Tale Riddles

Set 1

EMC 2723
©2004 by Evan-Moor Corp.

Fairy-Tale Riddles

Set 1

EMC 2723
©2004 by Evan-Moor Corp.

Fairy-Tale Riddles

Set 1

EMC 2723
©2004 by Evan-Moor Corp.

Fairy-Tale Riddles

Set 1

EMC 2723
©2004 by Evan-Moor Corp.

Fairy-Tale Riddles

Set 1

EMC 2723
©2004 by Evan-Moor Corp.

Fairy-Tale Riddles

Set 1

EMC 2723
©2004 by Evan-Moor Corp.

Fairy-Tale Riddles

Set 1

EMC 2723
©2004 by Evan-Moor Corp.

1

One day when I was fishing, I caught a magic fish. The fish granted my wishes until my wife became too greedy. Then we lost everything. Who am I?

2

We crept in at night to help a poor man and his wife. Who are we?

3

I needed a kiss from a princess to break a magic spell and turn me back into a prince. Who am I?

4

My husband caught a magic fish. I made my husband go ask the fish to make me ruler of the universe. This made the fish angry, and I lost everything. Who am I?

5

I was the ruler of my country. I made my daughter keep her promise to a frog. Who am I?

6

One morning, I was surprised to find that overnight someone had made a pair of shoes with the leather on my workbench. Who am I?

Fairy-Tale Riddles

Set 2

EMC 2723
©2004 by Evan-Moor Corp. .

Fairy-Tale Riddles

Set 2

EMC 2723
©2004 by Evan-Moor Corp. .

Fairy-Tale Riddles

Set 2

EMC 2723
©2004 by Evan-Moor Corp. .

Fairy-Tale Riddles

Set 2

EMC 2723
©2004 by Evan-Moor Corp. .

Fairy-Tale Riddles

Set 2

EMC 2723
©2004 by Evan-Moor Corp. .

Fairy-Tale Riddles

Set 2

EMC 2723
©2004 by Evan-Moor Corp. .

7

When our stepmother sent us into the woods, I dropped bread crumbs so my sister and I could find our way back home. Birds ate the bread crumbs. We were lost! Who am I?

8

My husband made tiny shoes, and I sewed tiny clothes for the tiny people who helped us. Who am I?

9

I pushed a wicked old witch into an oven and rescued my brother. Who am I?

10

I lost my golden ball down a well. A frog went into the well to get it for me. I was unkind to him, but my father made me keep the promise I had made to the frog. Who am I?

11

I lived in the sea. I granted the fisherman his wishes until his greedy wife asked for too much. Who am I?

12

I used a house made of cookies and candy to trick lost children. When they nibbled at my house, I would catch them. Who am I?

Fairy-Tale Riddles

Set 2

EMC 2723
©2004 by Evan-Moor Corp. .

Fairy-Tale Riddles

Set 2

EMC 2723
©2004 by Evan-Moor Corp. .

Fairy-Tale Riddles

Set 2

EMC 2723
©2004 by Evan-Moor Corp. .

Fairy-Tale Riddles

Set 2

EMC 2723
©2004 by Evan-Moor Corp. .

Fairy-Tale Riddles

Set 2

EMC 2723
©2004 by Evan-Moor Corp. .

Fairy-Tale Riddles

Set 2

EMC 2723
©2004 by Evan-Moor Corp. .

magic fish

frog prince

Gretel

shoemaker's wife

witch

Hansel

princess

shoemaker

fisherman

elves

king

fisherman's wife

Fairy-Tale Riddles

Set 2

EMC 2723
©2004 by Evan-Moor Corp.

Fairy-Tale Riddles

Set 2

EMC 2723
©2004 by Evan-Moor Corp.

Fairy-Tale Riddles

Set 2

EMC 2723
©2004 by Evan-Moor Corp.

Fairy-Tale Riddles

Set 2

EMC 2723
©2004 by Evan-Moor Corp.

Fairy-Tale Riddles

Set 2

EMC 2723
©2004 by Evan-Moor Corp.

Fairy-Tale Riddles

Set 2

EMC 2723
©2004 by Evan-Moor Corp.

Fairy-Tale Riddles

Set 2

EMC 2723
©2004 by Evan-Moor Corp.

Fairy-Tale Riddles

Set 2

EMC 2723
©2004 by Evan-Moor Corp.

Fairy-Tale Riddles

Set 2

EMC 2723
©2004 by Evan-Moor Corp.

Fairy-Tale Riddles

Set 2

EMC 2723
©2004 by Evan-Moor Corp.

Fairy-Tale Riddles

Set 2

EMC 2723
©2004 by Evan-Moor Corp.

Fairy-Tale Riddles

Set 2

EMC 2723
©2004 by Evan-Moor Corp.

Draw and Write

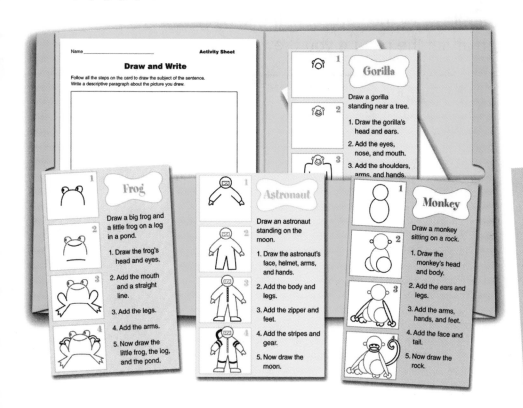 

Preparing the Center

1. Prepare a folder following the directions on page 3.

   Cover—page 73
   Student Directions—page 75
   Task Cards—pages 77–89

2. Reproduce a supply of the activity sheet on page 72. Place copies in the left-hand pocket of the folder.

Using the Center

1. The student selects a task card and an activity sheet.

2. Next, the student uses the drawing steps as guidance to draw the scene described in the sentence.

3. Then the student writes a paragraph to describe the picture.

Draw and Write

Follow all the steps on the card to draw the subject of the sentence.
Write a descriptive paragraph about the picture you drew.

Bonus: Add more details to the picture.

Draw and Write

Follow these steps:

1. Take an activity sheet and one drawing card from the folder.

2. Follow the drawing steps to draw the picture.

3. Write a descriptive paragraph about what you drew.

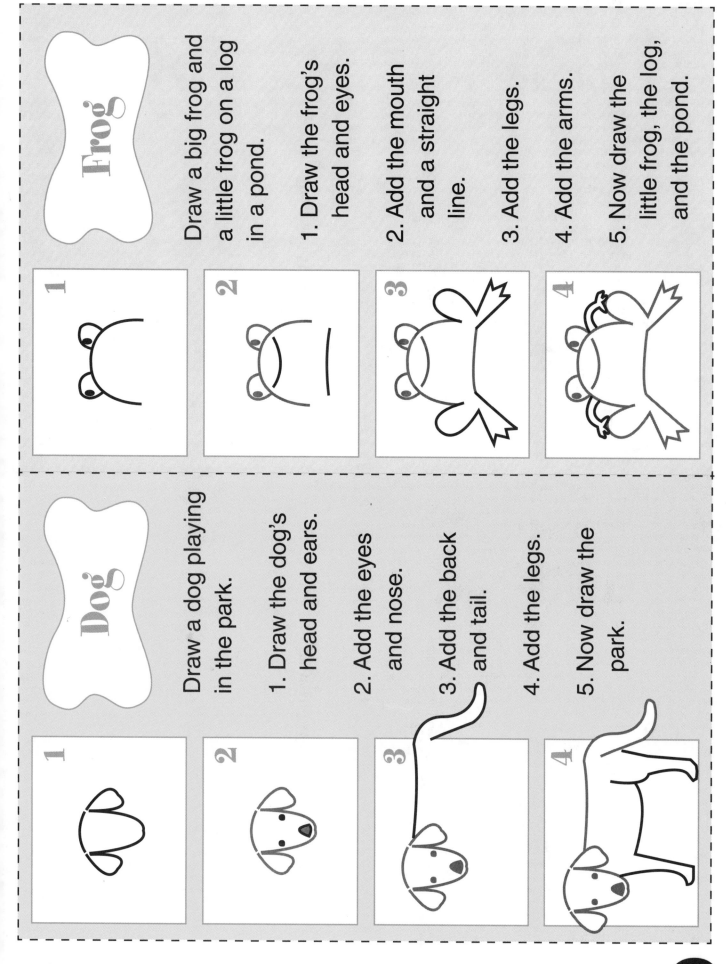

Frog

Draw a big frog and a little frog on a log in a pond.

1. Draw the frog's head and eyes.

2. Add the mouth and a straight line.

3. Add the legs.

4. Add the arms.

5. Now draw the little frog, the log, and the pond.

Dog

Draw a dog playing in the park.

1. Draw the dog's head and ears.

2. Add the eyes and nose.

3. Add the back and tail.

4. Add the legs.

5. Now draw the park.

Draw and Write

EMC 2723
©2004 by Evan-Moor Corp.

Draw and Write

EMC 2723
©2004 by Evan-Moor Corp.

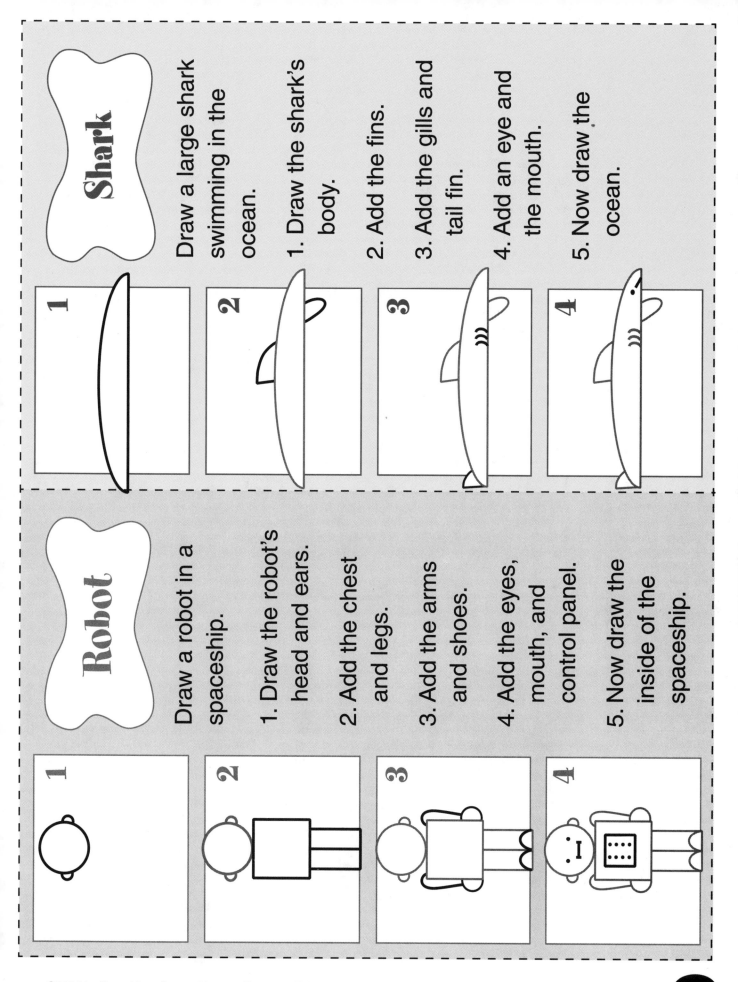

Shark

Draw a large shark swimming in the ocean.

1. Draw the shark's body.

2. Add the fins.

3. Add the gills and tail fin.

4. Add an eye and the mouth.

5. Now draw the ocean.

Robot

Draw a robot in a spaceship.

1. Draw the robot's head and ears.

2. Add the chest and legs.

3. Add the arms and shoes.

4. Add the eyes, mouth, and control panel.

5. Now draw the inside of the spaceship.

Draw and Write

©2004 by Evan-Moor Corp.
EMC 2723

Draw and Write

©2004 by Evan-Moor Corp.
EMC 2723

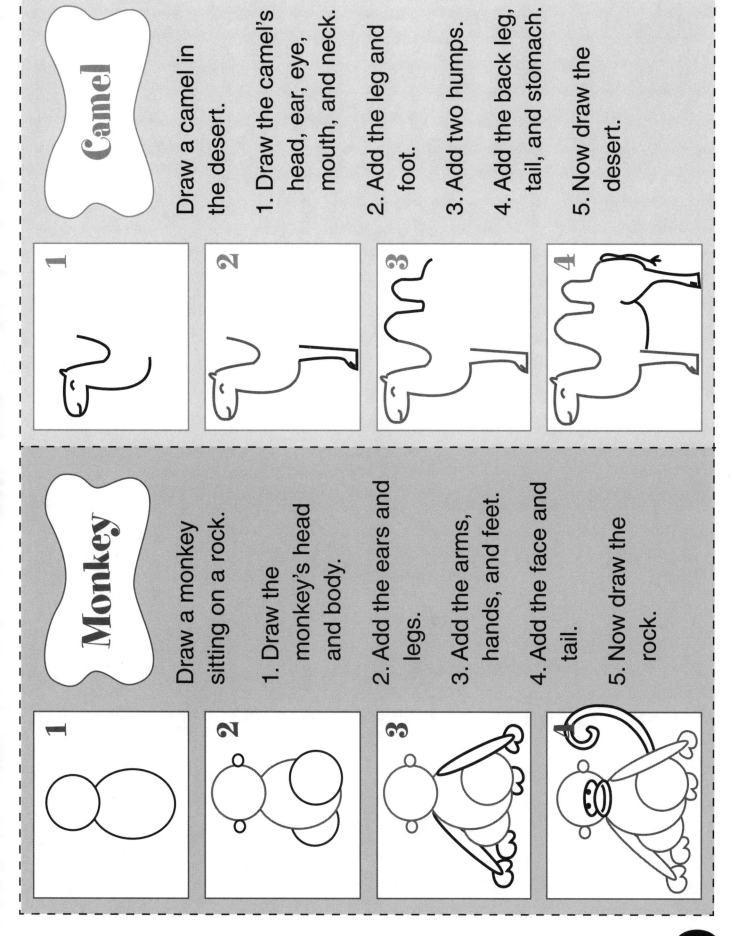

Camel

Draw a camel in the desert.

1. Draw the camel's head, ear, eye, mouth, and neck.

2. Add the leg and foot.

3. Add two humps.

4. Add the back leg, tail, and stomach.

5. Now draw the desert.

Monkey

Draw a monkey sitting on a rock.

1. Draw the monkey's head and body.

2. Add the ears and legs.

3. Add the arms, hands, and feet.

4. Add the face and tail.

5. Now draw the rock.

Draw and Write

©2004 by Evan-Moor Corp.
EMC 2723

Draw and Write

©2004 by Evan-Moor Corp.
EMC 2723

Helicopter

Draw a helicopter flying in the sky.

1. Draw the helicopter's cab.

2. Add the tail and the legs.

3. Add the propeller and the skid.

4. Add the window and the rotor.

5. Now draw the sky.

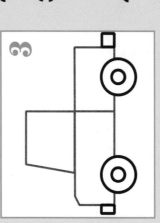
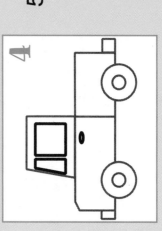

Pickup Truck

Draw a pickup truck carrying a large load.

1. Draw the truck's cab.

2. Add the body.

3. Add the bumpers and the tires.

4. Add the windows and door handle.

5. Now draw the large load.

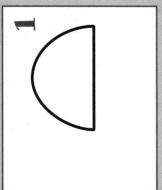

Draw and Write

©2004 by Evan-Moor Corp.

EMC 2723

Draw and Write

©2004 by Evan-Moor Corp.

EMC 2723

Astronaut

Draw an astronaut standing on the moon.

1. Draw the astronaut's face, helmet, arms, and hands.

2. Add the body and legs.

3. Add the zipper and feet.

4. Add the stripes and gear.

5. Now draw the moon.

Cowboy

Draw a cowboy with his favorite horse.

1. Draw the cowboy's face and hat.

2. Add the vest.

3. Add the legs and feet.

4. Add the arms.

5. Now draw his favorite horse.

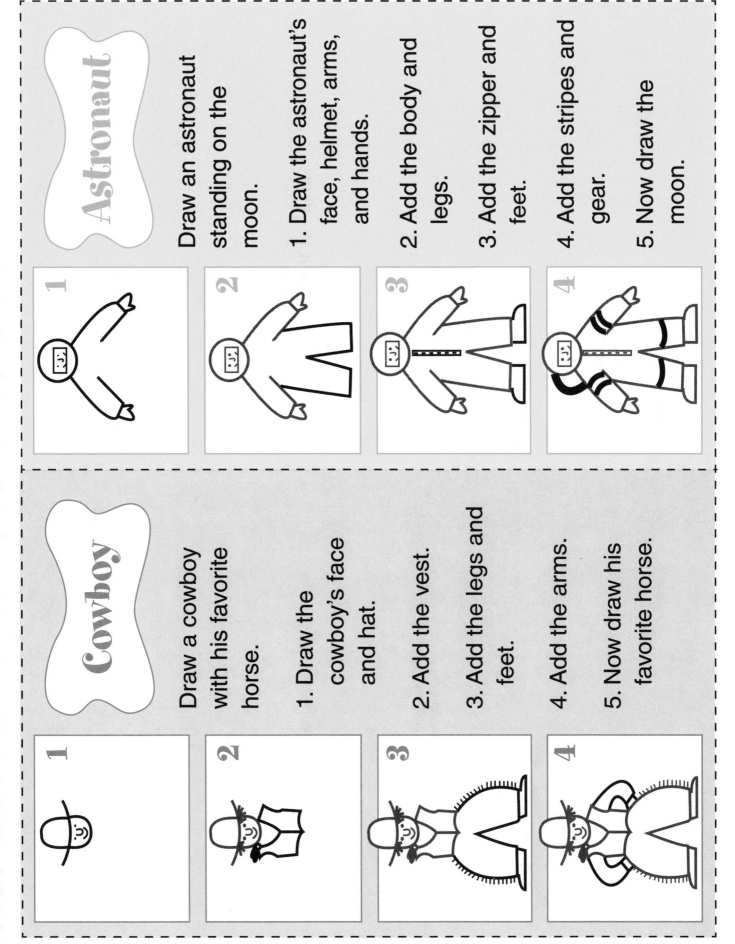

Draw and Write

EMC 2723
©2004 by Evan-Moor Corp.

Draw and Write

EMC 2723
©2004 by Evan-Moor Corp.

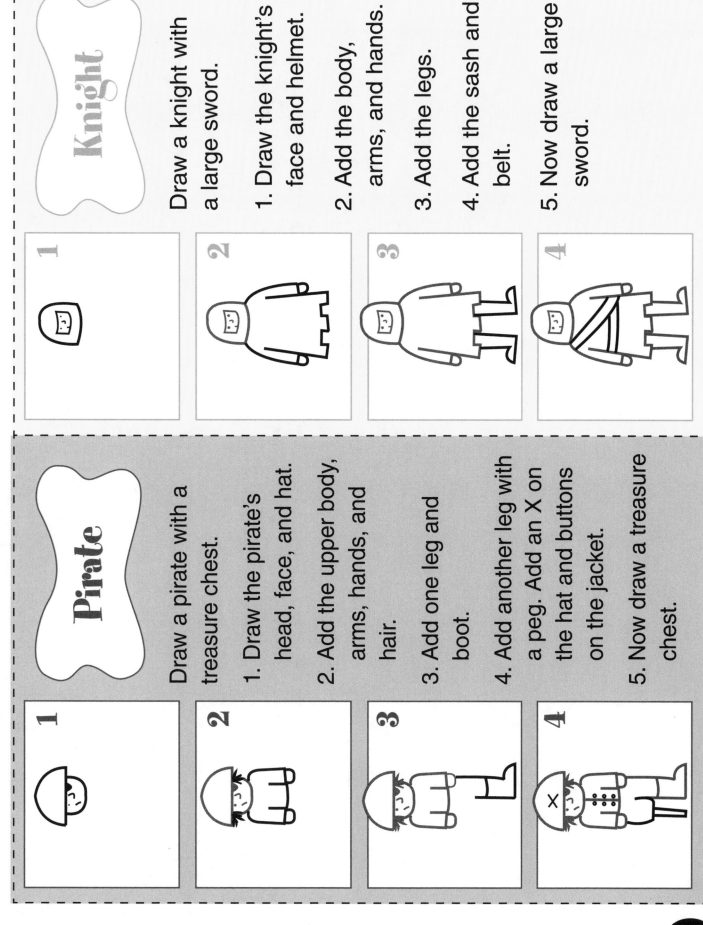

Knight

Draw a knight with a large sword.

1. Draw the knight's face and helmet.
2. Add the body, arms, and hands.
3. Add the legs.
4. Add the sash and belt.
5. Now draw a large sword.

Pirate

Draw a pirate with a treasure chest.

1. Draw the pirate's head, face, and hat.
2. Add the upper body, arms, hands, and hair.
3. Add one leg and boot.
4. Add another leg with a peg. Add an X on the hat and buttons on the jacket.
5. Now draw a treasure chest.

Draw and Write

EMC 2723
©2004 by Evan-Moor Corp.

Draw and Write

EMC 2723
©2004 by Evan-Moor Corp.

Cheerleader

Draw 2 cheerleaders with pompoms.

1. Draw the cheerleader's head, face, and hair.

2. Add the upper body, arms, and hands.

3. Add the skirt and pompoms.

4. Add the legs, socks, and shoes.

5. Now draw another cheerleader.

Gorilla

Draw a gorilla standing near a tree.

1. Draw the gorilla's head and ears.

2. Add the eyes, nose, and mouth.

3. Add the shoulders, arms, and hands.

4. Add the legs, feet, and stomach.

5. Now draw a tree.

Draw and Write

©2004 by Evan-Moor Corp.

EMC 2723

Draw and Write

©2004 by Evan-Moor Corp.

EMC 2723

Antonyms

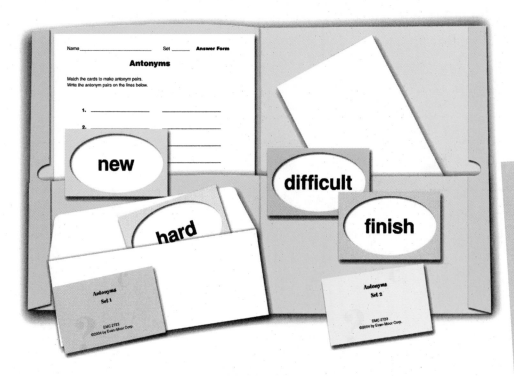

Preparing the Center

1. Prepare a folder following the directions on page 3.

   Cover—page 93
   Student Directions—page 95
   Task Cards—pages 97–103

2. Reproduce a supply of the answer form on page 92. Place copies in the left-hand pocket of the folder.

Using the Center

1. The student selects a set of task cards and writes the set number on the answer form.

2. Next, the student matches the task cards to create antonym pairs.

3. The student writes the antonym pairs on the answer form.

Antonyms

Match the cards to make antonym pairs.
Write the antonym pairs on the lines below.

1. _____   _____

2. _____   _____

3. _____   _____

4. _____   _____

5. _____   _____

6. _____   _____

7. _____   _____

8. _____   _____

Bonus: Choose a pair of words. On the back of this form, write a sentence using both words.

Literacy Centers—Take It to Your Seat • EMC 2723 • ©2004 by Evan-Moor Corp.

Antonyms

Antonyms

Antonyms are words that have opposite meanings.

near—far

back—front

stop—start

Follow these steps:

1. Choose a set of task cards. Write the set number on the answer form.

2. Match the cards to make antonym pairs.

3. Write the antonym pairs on the answer form.

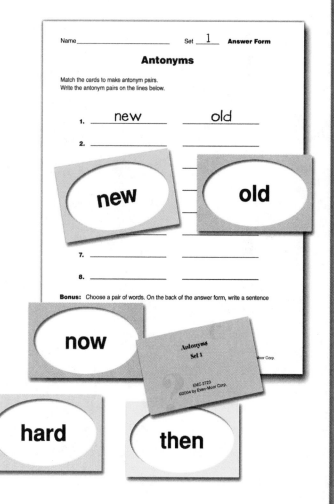

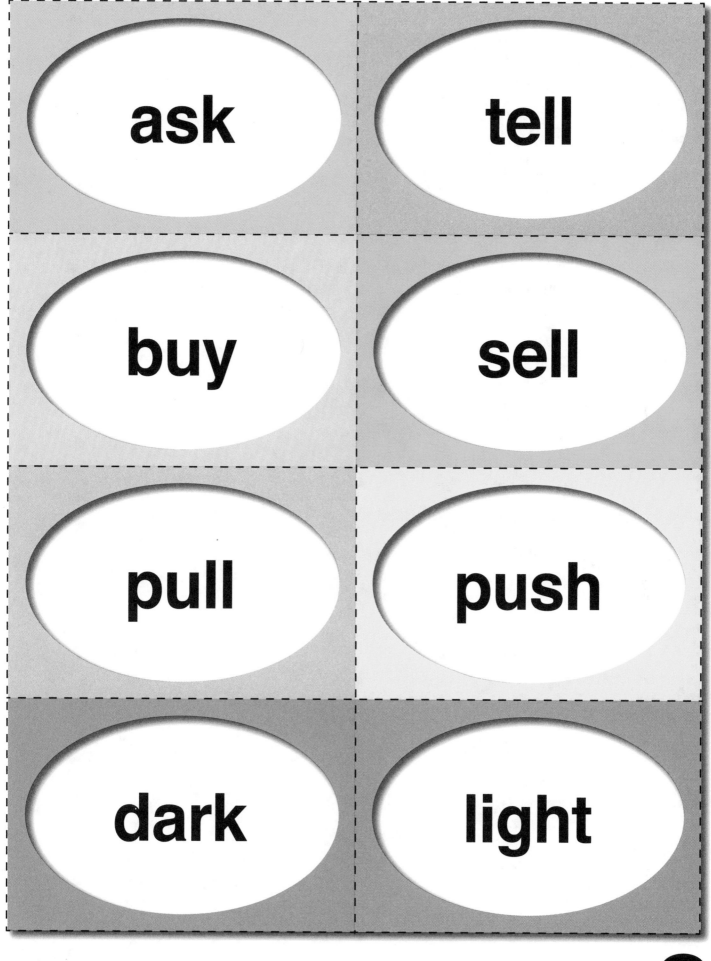

ask

tell

buy

sell

pull

push

dark

light

Antonyms

Set 1

Antonyms

Set 1

Antonyms

Set 1

Antonyms

Set 1

Antonyms

Set 1

Antonyms

Set 1

Antonyms

Set 1

Antonyms

Set 1

new	old
hard	soft
now	then
before	after

Antonyms

Set 1

Antonyms

Set 1

Antonyms

Set 1

Antonyms

Set 1

Antonyms

Set 1

Antonyms

Set 1

Antonyms

Set 1

Antonyms

Set 1

difficult

easy

finish

start

child

adult

morning

evening

Antonyms
Set 2

Antonyms
Set 2

Antonyms
Set 2

Antonyms
Set 2

Antonyms
Set 2

Antonyms
Set 2

Antonyms
Set 2

Antonyms
Set 2

follow

lead

false

true

break

repair

many

few

Antonyms

Set 2

EMC 2723
©2004 by Evan-Moor Corp.

Antonyms

Set 2

EMC 2723
©2004 by Evan-Moor Corp.

Antonyms

Set 2

EMC 2723
©2004 by Evan-Moor Corp.

Antonyms

Set 2

EMC 2723
©2004 by Evan-Moor Corp.

Antonyms

Set 2

EMC 2723
©2004 by Evan-Moor Corp.

Antonyms

Set 2

EMC 2723
©2004 by Evan-Moor Corp.

Antonyms

Set 2

EMC 2723
©2004 by Evan-Moor Corp.

Antonyms

Set 2

EMC 2723
©2004 by Evan-Moor Corp.

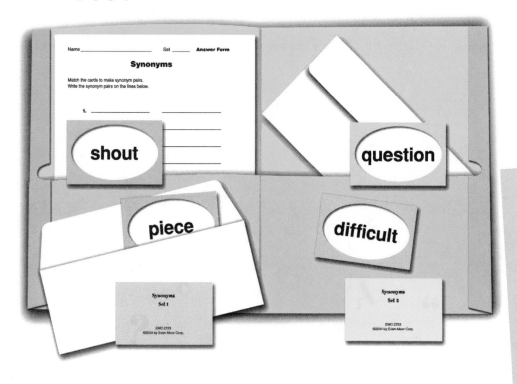

Preparing the Center

1. Prepare a folder following the directions on page 3.

   Cover—page 107
   Student Directions—page 109
   Task Cards—pages 111–117

2. Reproduce a supply of the answer form on page 106. Place copies in the left-hand pocket of the folder.

Using the Center

1. The student selects a set of task cards and writes the set number on the answer form.

2. Next, the student matches the task cards to create synonym pairs.

3. The student writes the synonym pairs on the answer form.

Synonyms

Match the cards to make synonym pairs.
Write the synonym pairs on the lines below.

1. _____   _____

2. _____   _____

3. _____   _____

4. _____   _____

5. _____   _____

6. _____   _____

7. _____   _____

8. _____   _____

Bonus: Choose a pair of words. On the back of this form, write a sentence using both words.

Literacy Centers—Take It to Your Seat • EMC 2723 • ©2004 by Evan-Moor Corp.

Synonyms

Synonyms are words that have about the same meaning.

car—auto

sea—ocean

night—evening

Follow these steps:

1. Choose a set of task cards. Write the set number on the answer form.

2. Match the cards to make synonym pairs.

3. Write the synonym pairs on the answer form.

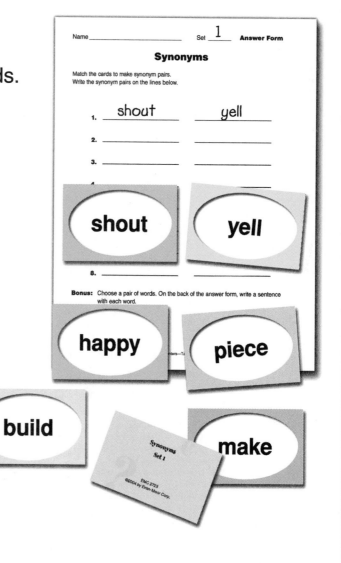

begin

start

shout

yell

part

piece

gift

present

Synonyms
Set 1

Synonyms
Set 1

Synonyms
Set 1

Synonyms
Set 1

Synonyms
Set 1

Synonyms
Set 1

Synonyms
Set 1

Synonyms
Set 1

make

build

happy

glad

go

leave

fast

quick

Synonyms
Set 1

Synonyms
Set 1

Synonyms
Set 1

Synonyms
Set 1

Synonyms
Set 1

Synonyms
Set 1

Synonyms
Set 1

Synonyms
Set 1

hard

difficult

ask

question

find

locate

fragile

delicate

Synonyms
Set 2

EMC 2723
©2004 by Evan-Moor Corp.

Synonyms
Set 2

EMC 2723
©2004 by Evan-Moor Corp.

Synonyms
Set 2

EMC 2723
©2004 by Evan-Moor Corp.

Synonyms
Set 2

EMC 2723
©2004 by Evan-Moor Corp.

Synonyms
Set 2

EMC 2723
©2004 by Evan-Moor Corp.

Synonyms
Set 2

EMC 2723
©2004 by Evan-Moor Corp.

Synonyms
Set 2

EMC 2723
©2004 by Evan-Moor Corp.

Synonyms
Set 2

EMC 2723
©2004 by Evan-Moor Corp.

brave

daring

allow

permit

all

whole

buy

purchase

Synonyms
Set 2

EMC 2723
©2004 by Evan-Moor Corp.

Synonyms
Set 2

EMC 2723
©2004 by Evan-Moor Corp.

Synonyms
Set 2

EMC 2723
©2004 by Evan-Moor Corp.

Synonyms
Set 2

EMC 2723
©2004 by Evan-Moor Corp.

Synonyms
Set 2

EMC 2723
©2004 by Evan-Moor Corp.

Synonyms
Set 2

EMC 2723
©2004 by Evan-Moor Corp.

Synonyms
Set 2

EMC 2723
©2004 by Evan-Moor Corp.

Synonyms
Set 2

EMC 2723
©2004 by Evan-Moor Corp.

As Busy as a Bee!

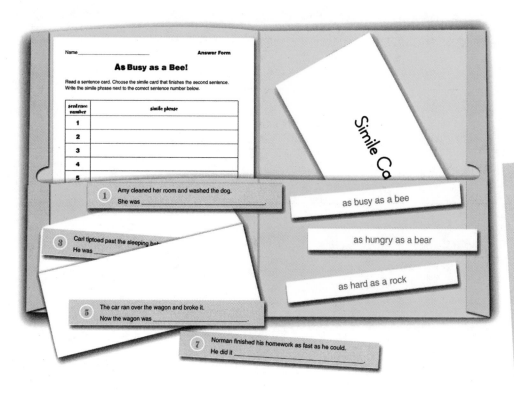

Preparing the Center

1. Prepare a folder following the directions on page 3.

   Cover—page 121
   Student Directions—page 123
   Task Cards—pages 125 and 127

2. Reproduce a supply of the answer form on page 120. Place copies in the left-hand pocket of the folder.

Using the Center

1. The student chooses a sentence card and reads the pair of sentences.

2. The student finds the correct simile card and completes the second sentence.

3. On the answer form, the student writes the simile next to the correct sentence number.

As Busy as a Bee!

Read a sentence card. Choose the simile card that finishes the second sentence. Write the simile phrase next to the correct sentence number below.

sentence number	simile phrase
1	
2	
3	
4	
5	
6	
7	
8	
9	
10	

Bonus: Pick one of the phrase cards. Use it in a new sentence. Write the sentence on the back of this form.

The children were as busy as bees.

As Busy as a Bee!

A **simile** is a way of comparing two things. A simile uses the words **like** or **as**.

After playing ball in the hot sun, I felt as dry as a bone.

We couldn't have finished the job without John's help. He worked like a horse all day.

Follow these steps:

1. Read a sentence card.

2. Choose the simile card that completes the second sentence.

3. Write the simile phrase next to the correct sentence number on the answer form.

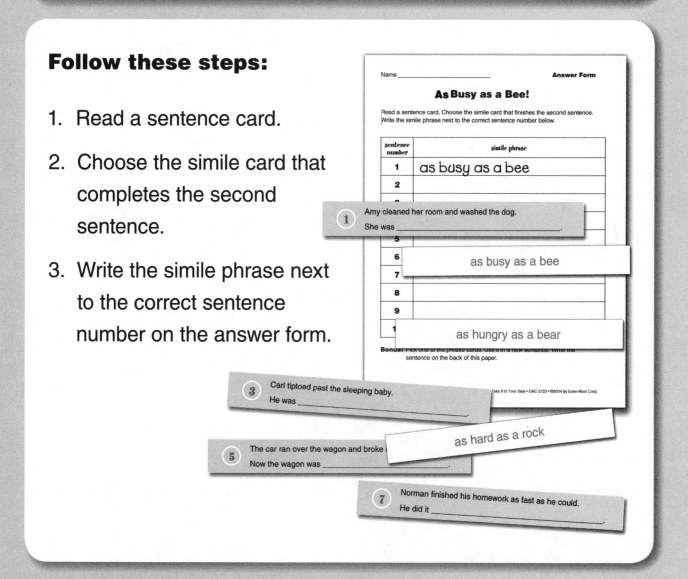

124

1 Amy cleaned her room and washed the dog.

She was _____.

2 Matt gobbled up his cereal and milk.

He was _____.

3 Carl tiptoed past the sleeping baby.

He was _____.

4 Kim's kitten did not weigh very much.

The kitten was _____.

5 The car ran over the wagon and broke it.

Now the wagon was _____.

6 Jon's little sister talked all the time.

Father said she _____.

7 Norman finished his homework as fast as he could.

He did it _____.

8 Susan found it hard to sleep on the camping trip.

The ground was _____.

9 Pete washed the car windows.

Now they _____.

10 The dishes on the table rattle when he crosses the room.

He _____.

As Busy as a Bee!

EMC 2723
©2004 by Evan-Moor Corp.

As Busy as a Bee!

EMC 2723
©2004 by Evan-Moor Corp.

As Busy as a Bee!

EMC 2723
©2004 by Evan-Moor Corp.

As Busy as a Bee!

EMC 2723
©2004 by Evan-Moor Corp.

As Busy as a Bee!

EMC 2723
©2004 by Evan-Moor Corp.

As Busy as a Bee!

EMC 2723
©2004 by Evan-Moor Corp.

As Busy as a Bee!

EMC 2723
©2004 by Evan-Moor Corp.

As Busy as a Bee!

EMC 2723
©2004 by Evan-Moor Corp.

As Busy as a Bee!

EMC 2723
©2004 by Evan-Moor Corp.

As Busy as a Bee!

EMC 2723
©2004 by Evan-Moor Corp.

as busy as a bee

as quiet as a mouse

as hungry as a bear

as light as a feather

as flat as a pancake

as hard as a rock

as quick as a wink

chattered like a monkey

sparkled like diamonds

walks like an elephant

As Busy as a Bee!

EMC 2723
©2004 by Evan-Moor Corp.

As Busy as a Bee!

EMC 2723
©2004 by Evan-Moor Corp.

As Busy as a Bee!

EMC 2723
©2004 by Evan-Moor Corp.

As Busy as a Bee!

EMC 2723
©2004 by Evan-Moor Corp.

As Busy as a Bee!

EMC 2723
©2004 by Evan-Moor Corp.

As Busy as a Bee!

EMC 2723
©2004 by Evan-Moor Corp.

As Busy as a Bee!

EMC 2723
©2004 by Evan-Moor Corp.

As Busy as a Bee!

EMC 2723
©2004 by Evan-Moor Corp.

As Busy as a Bee!

EMC 2723
©2004 by Evan-Moor Corp.

As Busy as a Bee!

EMC 2723
©2004 by Evan-Moor Corp.

Top Ten

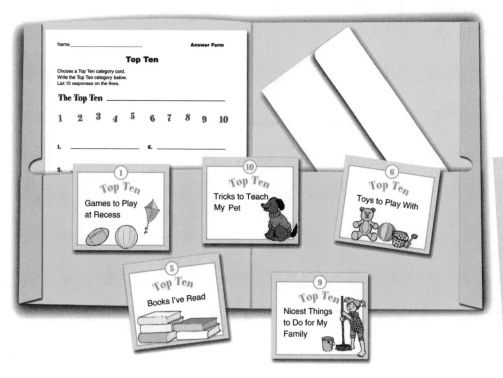

Preparing the Center

1. Prepare a folder following the directions on page 3.

   Cover—page 131
   Student Directions—page 133
   Task Cards—pages 135 and 137

2. Reproduce a supply of the answer form on page 130. Place copies in the left-hand pocket of the folder.

3. Allow students time to complete the bonus activity.

Using the Center

1. The student selects one of the Top Ten category cards and an answer form.

2. The student lists 10 responses on the answer form.

Top Ten

Choose a Top Ten category card.
Write the Top Ten category below.
List 10 responses on the lines.

The Top Ten _____

1   2   3   4   5   6   7   8   9   10

1. _____

2. _____

3. _____

4. _____

5. _____

6. _____

7. _____

8. _____

9. _____

10. _____

Bonus: Have 10 classmates put a check mark next to their favorite answer
from your Top Ten list.

Top Ten

A " j !

c ? k

G " y

Q S b

Top Ten

A **Top Ten** list is a list with items or ideas numbered in the order of how much you like them.

Number 1 = My most favorite out of all 10

Number 10 = My least favorite out of all 10

Follow these steps:

1. Choose a Top Ten category card.

2. Write the Top Ten category on the answer form.

3. List 10 responses on the answer form.

1

Top Ten

Games to Play
at Recess

2

Top Ten

Best Snacks

3

Top Ten

Things to Do on
a Rainy Day

4

Top Ten

Super
Vacations

5

Top Ten

Books I've Read

6

Top Ten

Toys to Play With

Top Ten

EMC 2723
©2004 by Evan-Moor Corp.

Top Ten

EMC 2723
©2004 by Evan-Moor Corp.

Top Ten

EMC 2723
©2004 by Evan-Moor Corp.

Top Ten

EMC 2723
©2004 by Evan-Moor Corp.

Top Ten

EMC 2723
©2004 by Evan-Moor Corp.

Top Ten

EMC 2723
©2004 by Evan-Moor Corp.

7

Top Ten

Heroes

8

Top Ten

Birthday Presents

9

Top Ten

Nicest Things to Do for My Family

10

Top Ten

Tricks to Teach My Pet

11

Top Ten

Excuses for Not Doing My Homework

12

Top Ten

Television Shows to Watch

Top Ten

EMC 2723
©2004 by Evan-Moor Corp.

Top Ten

EMC 2723
©2004 by Evan-Moor Corp.

Top Ten

EMC 2723
©2004 by Evan-Moor Corp.

Top Ten

EMC 2723
©2004 by Evan-Moor Corp.

Top Ten

EMC 2723
©2004 by Evan-Moor Corp.

Top Ten

EMC 2723
©2004 by Evan-Moor Corp.

It's in the Mail

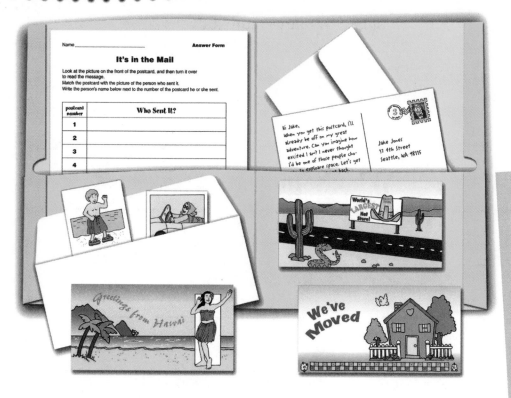
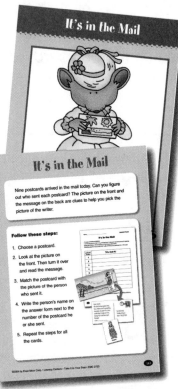

Preparing the Center

1. Prepare a folder following the directions on page 3.

   Cover—page 141
   Student Directions—page 143
   Task Cards—pages 145–151

2. Reproduce a supply of the answer form on page 140. Place copies in the left-hand pocket of the folder.

Using the Center

1. The student takes an answer form and selects a postcard.

2. The student looks at the picture on the postcard and reads the message on the back.

3. Next, the student matches the postcard with the picture of the person who sent it.

4. On the answer form, the student writes the sender's name next to the number of the postcard he or she sent.

It's in the Mail

Look at the picture on the front of the postcard, and then turn it over
to read the message.
Match the postcard with the picture of the person who sent it.
Write the person's name next to the number of the postcard he or she sent.

postcard number	Who Sent It?
1	
2	
3	
4	
5	
6	
7	
8	
9	

Bonus: On the back of this form, write an answer to one of the postcards.

It's in the Mail

Nine postcards arrived in the mail today. Can you figure out who sent each postcard? The picture on the front and the message on the back are clues to help you pick the picture of the writer.

Follow these steps:

1. Choose a postcard.

2. Look at the picture on the front. Then turn it over and read the message.

3. Match the postcard with the picture of the person who sent it.

4. Write the person's name on the answer form next to the number of the postcard he or she sent.

5. Repeat the steps for all the cards.

Dear Scott,

We are having a good time. Your father and I go surfing every day. We went to a luau yesterday. I hope you are having fun with Nana and Gramps.

Love, _____

Scott Brown
15 Elm Street
Apex, NC 00001

Dear Mom & Dad,

I was scared when I first got here. Now I am having so much fun! We go for hikes and swim. We paddle canoes. At night, we sing songs and tell stories around the campfire.

Love, _____

Mr. & Mrs. James Dunn
88 Downing Street
Little, CO 00002

Hi Jake,

When you get this postcard, I'll already be off on my great adventure. Can you imagine how excited I am? I never thought I'd be one of those people chosen to explore space. Let's get together when I get back.

Your friend, _____

Jake Jones
17 4th Street
Seattle, WA 00003

Dear Matt,
I am having a good time here at the beach. It is fun to wade in the water. I built a huge sand castle yesterday. Maybe you can come with me next time.
Your brother, _____

Matt Joseph
60 Grand Blvd.
San Marcos, TX 00004

Howdy partner,
I hear you are coming to spend some time here at the ranch. Your room is ready and waiting. Pack your boots and hurry on down.
See you soon, _____

Jessie Brooks
150 Lake Ave.
Modesto, CA 00005

To Sally and Sam,
I'm having fun zooming down the highway in my new car. Every day I see something exciting. Today I saw a store shaped like a giant cowboy hat. This has been the best trip ever!
From, _____

Sally and Sam Smith
261 Ramona Court
Carmel, CA 00006

Dear Carlos,
Thank you for taking me to the circus with you. I had a great time. The clowns were so funny! I really liked the acrobats, too.
Your friend, _____

Carlos Cruz
300 Rios Ave.
Cairo, IL 00007

Dear Bobby,
You are invited to my house for a sleepover. We can pitch a tent in the backyard and sleep outside. Ask your mother and father. I hope they say "yes."
Your friend, _____

Robert Watson
111 West Street
Hanover, MA 00008

Dear Ann and Arnold,
We have moved to a new house. I think you two will like it. This is our new address. Come for a visit as soon as you can.
Best wishes, _____

Ann and Arnold Evans
18 Crest Drive
Salem, OR 00009

Mother

Maggie

Astronaut Bill

George

Cowboy Bob

Aunt Suzie

Tanisha

Ronnie

Grandma and Grandpa

It's in the Mail

EMC 2723
©2004 by Evan-Moor Corp.

It's in the Mail

EMC 2723
©2004 by Evan-Moor Corp.

It's in the Mail

EMC 2723
©2004 by Evan-Moor Corp.

It's in the Mail

EMC 2723
©2004 by Evan-Moor Corp.

It's in the Mail

EMC 2723
©2004 by Evan-Moor Corp.

It's in the Mail

EMC 2723
©2004 by Evan-Moor Corp.

It's in the Mail

EMC 2723
©2004 by Evan-Moor Corp.

It's in the Mail

EMC 2723
©2004 by Evan-Moor Corp.

It's in the Mail

EMC 2723
©2004 by Evan-Moor Corp.

They Sound the Same

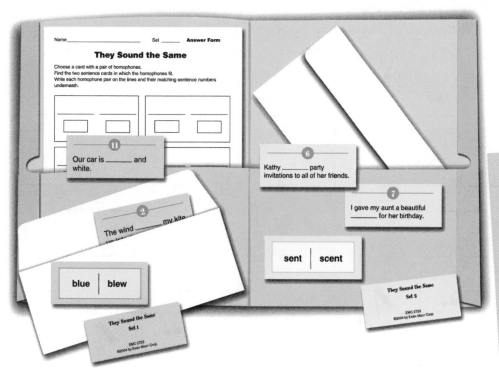

Preparing the Center

1. Prepare a folder following the directions on page 3.

   Cover—page 155
   Student Directions—page 157
   Task Cards—pages 159–163

2. Reproduce a supply of the answer form on page 154. Place copies in the left-hand pocket of the folder.

Using the Center

1. The student selects a set of task cards and writes the set number on the answer form.

2. The student chooses a card with a homophone pair.

3. Next, the student finds the two sentence cards in which the homophones fit.

4. On the answer form, the student writes each homophone pair and their matching sentence numbers.

They Sound the Same

Choose a card with a pair of homophones.

Find the two sentence cards in which the homophones fit.

Write each homophone pair on the lines and their matching sentence numbers underneath.

Bonus: Pick one pair of homophones below. On the back of this form, write two sentences to show what they mean.

through	threw	ate	eight	would	wood

They Sound the Same

Homophones are words that sound the same but are spelled differently and have different meanings.

break — to come apart
The earthquake caused the vase to fall and break.

brake — a device used to slow or stop movement
Dad used the emergency brake to stop the car.

Follow these steps:

1. Choose a set of task cards. Write the set number on the answer form.

2. Choose a card with a pair of homophones.

3. Find the two sentence cards in which the homophones fit.

4. Write each word pair and their matching sentence numbers on the answer form.

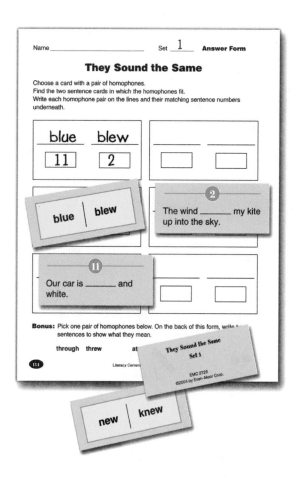

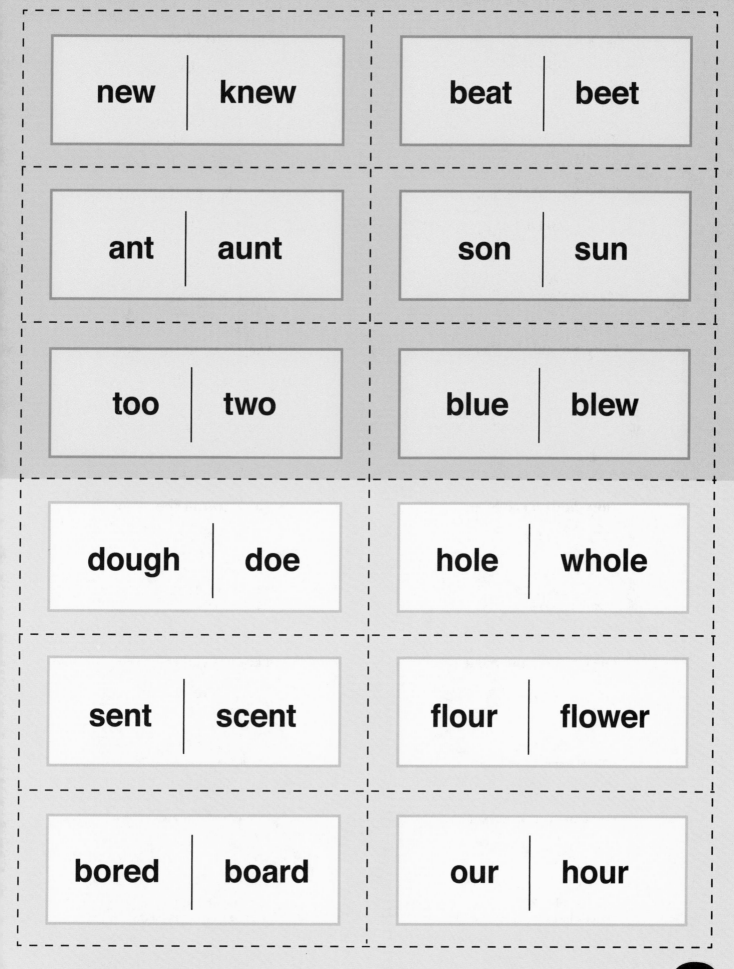

new	knew	beat	beet
ant	aunt	son	sun
too	two	blue	blew
dough	doe	hole	whole
sent	scent	flour	flower
bored	board	our	hour

They Sound the Same
Set 1

EMC 2723
©2004 by Evan-Moor Corp.

They Sound the Same
Set 1

EMC 2723
©2004 by Evan-Moor Corp.

They Sound the Same
Set 1

EMC 2723
©2004 by Evan-Moor Corp.

They Sound the Same
Set 1

EMC 2723
©2004 by Evan-Moor Corp.

They Sound the Same
Set 1

EMC 2723
©2004 by Evan-Moor Corp.

They Sound the Same
Set 1

EMC 2723
©2004 by Evan-Moor Corp.

They Sound the Same
Set 2

EMC 2723
©2004 by Evan-Moor Corp.

They Sound the Same
Set 2

EMC 2723
©2004 by Evan-Moor Corp.

They Sound the Same
Set 2

EMC 2723
©2004 by Evan-Moor Corp.

They Sound the Same
Set 2

EMC 2723
©2004 by Evan-Moor Corp.

They Sound the Same
Set 2

EMC 2723
©2004 by Evan-Moor Corp.

They Sound the Same
Set 2

EMC 2723
©2004 by Evan-Moor Corp.

1

Don't _____ that drum in the house.

2

The wind _____ my kite up into the sky.

3

An _____ bit me on my foot.

4

I have _____ pet dogs.

5

Do you like your _____ shoes?

6

She _____ how to bake a cake.

7

Her _____ came for a visit.

8

The _____ is shining in the sky.

9

Would you like to go to the park, _____?

10

Mr. Lee has one _____ and one daughter.

11

Our car is _____ and white.

12

A _____ is good to eat.

They Sound the Same

Set 1

EMC 2723
©2004 by Evan-Moor Corp.

They Sound the Same

Set 1

EMC 2723
©2004 by Evan-Moor Corp.

They Sound the Same

Set 1

EMC 2723
©2004 by Evan-Moor Corp.

They Sound the Same

Set 1

EMC 2723
©2004 by Evan-Moor Corp.

They Sound the Same

Set 1

EMC 2723
©2004 by Evan-Moor Corp.

They Sound the Same

Set 1

EMC 2723
©2004 by Evan-Moor Corp.

They Sound the Same

Set 1

EMC 2723
©2004 by Evan-Moor Corp.

They Sound the Same

Set 1

EMC 2723
©2004 by Evan-Moor Corp.

They Sound the Same

Set 1

EMC 2723
©2004 by Evan-Moor Corp.

They Sound the Same

Set 1

EMC 2723
©2004 by Evan-Moor Corp.

They Sound the Same

Set 1

EMC 2723
©2004 by Evan-Moor Corp.

They Sound the Same

Set 1

EMC 2723
©2004 by Evan-Moor Corp.

1

Kim helped Grandma make cookie _____.

2

Sally complained, "I'm _____. I don't have anything to do."

3

Have you seen _____ new car yet?

4

The frightened skunk sprayed a terrible _____ on the fox.

5

The mouse ran and hid in the _____.

6

Kathy _____ party invitations to all of her friends.

7

I gave my aunt a beautiful _____ for her birthday.

8

The fawn walked behind the _____.

9

The baker needs to buy _____ before he can bake bread.

10

He ate the _____ pizza!

11

Mark nailed a _____ on the fence to fix it.

12

In one _____, we will catch the airplane for Hawaii.

They Sound the Same

Set 2

EMC 2723
©2004 by Evan-Moor Corp.

They Sound the Same

Set 2

EMC 2723
©2004 by Evan-Moor Corp.

They Sound the Same

Set 2

EMC 2723
©2004 by Evan-Moor Corp.

They Sound the Same

Set 2

EMC 2723
©2004 by Evan-Moor Corp.

They Sound the Same

Set 2

EMC 2723
©2004 by Evan-Moor Corp.

They Sound the Same

Set 2

EMC 2723
©2004 by Evan-Moor Corp.

They Sound the Same

Set 2

EMC 2723
©2004 by Evan-Moor Corp.

They Sound the Same

Set 2

EMC 2723
©2004 by Evan-Moor Corp.

They Sound the Same

Set 2

EMC 2723
©2004 by Evan-Moor Corp.

They Sound the Same

Set 2

EMC 2723
©2004 by Evan-Moor Corp.

They Sound the Same

Set 2

EMC 2723
©2004 by Evan-Moor Corp.

More Than One

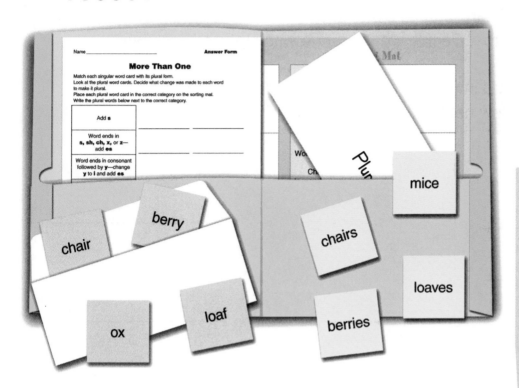

Preparing the Center

1. Prepare a folder following the directions on page 3.

   Cover—page 167
   Student Directions—page 169
   Sorting Mat—pages 171 and 173
   Task Cards—pages 175 and 177

2. Tape the two pages of the sorting mat (pages 171 and 173) together and laminate them. Fold the mat in half to fit in the folder.

3. Reproduce a supply of the answer form on page 166. Place copies in the left-hand pocket of the folder.

Using the Center

1. The student takes the task cards, sorting mat, and answer form.

2. The student selects each singular word card and matches it with its plural form.

3. Next, the student looks at each plural word card and determines what change was made in order to make the word plural.

4. The student then places each plural word card in the correct category on the sorting mat.

5. On the answer form, the student writes the plural words next to the correct category.

More Than One

Match each singular word card with its plural form.
Look at the plural word cards. Decide what change was made to each word
to make it plural.
Place each plural word card in the correct category on the sorting mat.
Write the plural words below next to the correct category.

Add **s**	
Word ends in **s, sh, ch, x,** or **z**— add **es**	
Word ends in consonant followed by **y**—change **y** to **i** and add **es**	
Word ends in vowel followed by **y**—add **s**	
Word ends in **f**—change **f** to **v** and add **es**	
Some nouns form a plural by taking on an irregular spelling: **goose–geese**	

Bonus: Write the plural form of these words on the back of this form.

coat   box   baby   toy   wife   zero   man   elf

 Literacy Centers—Take It to Your Seat • EMC 2723 • ©2004 by Evan-Moor Corp.

More Than One

A **singular** noun names one person, place, thing, or idea.
A **plural** noun names more than one person, place, thing, or idea.
Changes are usually made to the spelling of a singular noun to make it plural.

Singular	Plural	Singular	Plural
man	men	lunch	lunches
park	parks	cherry	cherries

Follow these steps:

1. Match each singular word card with its plural form.

2. Then look at the plural word cards. Decide what change was made to each word to make it plural.

3. Place each plural word card in the correct category on the sorting mat.

4. On the answer form, write each plural word next to the correct category.

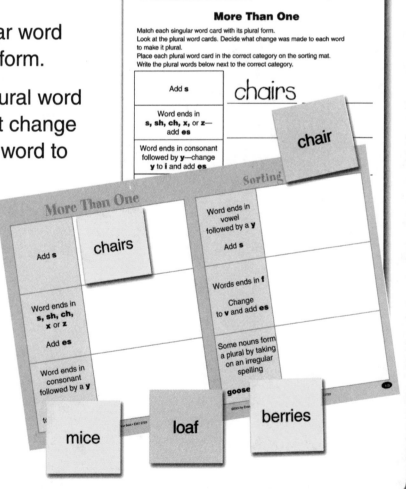

Add **s**	
Word ends in **s, sh, ch, x,** or **z** Add **es**	
Word ends in consonant followed by **y** Change **y** to **i** and add **es**	

Word ends in vowel followed by **y** Add **s**	
Word ends in **f** Change **f** to **v** and add **es**	
Some nouns form a plural by taking on an irregular spelling **goose–geese**	

chair	ship	fox
bench	city	berry
loaf	calf	boy
monkey	mouse	ox

More Than One

EMC 2723
©2004 by Evan-Moor Corp.

More Than One

EMC 2723
©2004 by Evan-Moor Corp.

More Than One

EMC 2723
©2004 by Evan-Moor Corp.

More Than One

EMC 2723
©2004 by Evan-Moor Corp.

More Than One

EMC 2723
©2004 by Evan-Moor Corp.

More Than One

EMC 2723
©2004 by Evan-Moor Corp.

More Than One

EMC 2723
©2004 by Evan-Moor Corp.

More Than One

EMC 2723
©2004 by Evan-Moor Corp.

More Than One

EMC 2723
©2004 by Evan-Moor Corp.

More Than One

EMC 2723
©2004 by Evan-Moor Corp.

More Than One

EMC 2723
©2004 by Evan-Moor Corp.

More Than One

EMC 2723
©2004 by Evan-Moor Corp.

chairs	ships	foxes
benches	cities	berries
loaves	calves	boys
monkeys	mice	oxen

More Than One

More Than One

More Than One

More Than One

More Than One

More Than One

More Than One

More Than One

More Than One

More Than One

More Than One

More Than One

More Than One Meaning

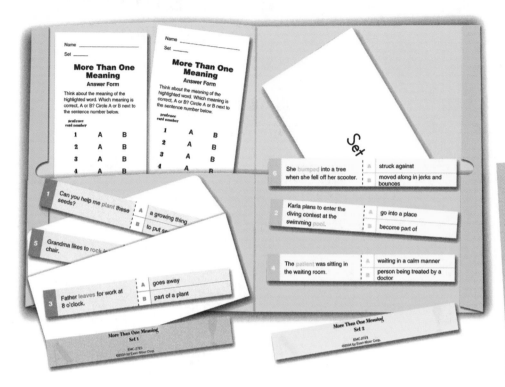

Preparing the Center

1. Prepare a folder following the directions on page 3.

   Cover—page 181
   Student Directions—page 183
   Task Cards—pages 185 and 187

2. Reproduce a supply of the answer form on page 180. Place copies in the left-hand pocket of the folder.

Using the Center

1. The student selects a set of task cards and writes the set number on the answer form.

2. The student reads each sentence card and determines how the highlighted word is used.

3. On the answer form, the student circles definition A or definition B to indicate how the multiple-meaning word is being used.

Name _____

Set _____

More Than One Meaning
Answer Form

Think about the meaning of the highlighted word. Which meaning is correct, A or B? Circle A or B next to the sentence number below.

sentence card number

1   **A**   **B**

2   **A**   **B**

3   **A**   **B**

4   **A**   **B**

5   **A**   **B**

6   **A**   **B**

7   **A**   **B**

8   **A**   **B**

9   **A**   **B**

Bonus: Select one word from the list below. On the back of this form, write sentences to show two different meanings for the word.

mean   slide   ring   whistle

Name _____

Set _____

More Than One Meaning
Answer Form

Think about the meaning of the highlighted word. Which meaning is correct, A or B? Circle A or B next to the sentence number below.

sentence card number

1   **A**   **B**

2   **A**   **B**

3   **A**   **B**

4   **A**   **B**

5   **A**   **B**

6   **A**   **B**

7   **A**   **B**

8   **A**   **B**

9   **A**   **B**

Bonus: Select one word from the list below. On the back of this form, write sentences to show two different meanings for the word.

mean   slide   ring   whistle

Literacy Centers—Take It to Your Seat • EMC 2723 • ©2004 by Evan-Moor Corp.

More Than One Meaning

More Than One Meaning

Many words have more than one meaning.
These words are called **multiple-meaning words**.

Follow these steps:

1. Choose a set of task cards. Write the set number on the answer form.

2. Read a sentence card and think about the meaning of the highlighted word.

3. On the answer form, circle definition A or definition B to show the correct meaning.

4. Repeat the steps for all of the cards.

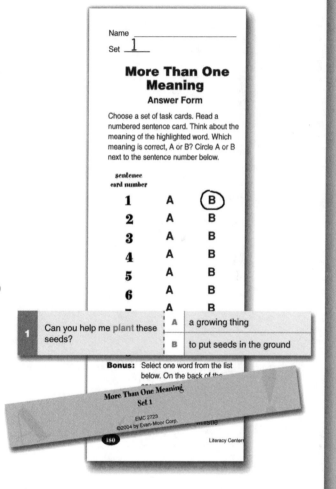

1	Can you help me **plant** these seeds?	**A**	a growing thing
		B	to put seeds in the ground
2	Put the toys in the **trunk**.	**A**	a storage container
		B	an elephant's nose
3	Father **leaves** for work at 8 o'clock.	**A**	goes away
		B	part of a plant
4	Did you **watch** the game on TV?	**A**	something to use to tell time
		B	to look at something
5	Grandma likes to **rock** in her chair.	**A**	to move back and forth
		B	a stone
6	I hurt my **neck** when I fell down.	**A**	a part of your body
		B	a part of a shirt
7	I threw a **stick** for my dog to catch.	**A**	to glue something to paper
		B	a piece of wood
8	The fish looked for food on the creek **bed**.	**A**	the ground under a body of water
		B	something to sleep on
9	Did you hear something **bark**?	**A**	the outside cover on a tree
		B	the sound a dog makes

More Than One Meaning
Set 1

EMC 2723
©2004 by Evan-Moor Corp.

More Than One Meaning
Set 1

EMC 2723
©2004 by Evan-Moor Corp.

More Than One Meaning
Set 1

EMC 2723
©2004 by Evan-Moor Corp.

More Than One Meaning
Set 1

EMC 2723
©2004 by Evan-Moor Corp.

More Than One Meaning
Set 1

EMC 2723
©2004 by Evan-Moor Corp.

More Than One Meaning
Set 1

EMC 2723
©2004 by Evan-Moor Corp.

More Than One Meaning
Set 1

EMC 2723
©2004 by Evan-Moor Corp.

More Than One Meaning
Set 1

EMC 2723
©2004 by Evan-Moor Corp.

More Than One Meaning
Set 1

EMC 2723
©2004 by Evan-Moor Corp.

1	Sam tossed a coin into the wishing well.	**A**	in good health
		B	water from underground
2	Karla plans to enter the diving contest at the swimming pool.	**A**	go into a place
		B	become part of
3	I'm going to plant a garden this spring.	**A**	the season after winter
		B	a small stream of water coming from the ground
4	The patient was sitting in the waiting room.	**A**	waiting in a calm manner
		B	a person being treated by a doctor
5	Marcus rode his bike around the block.	**A**	to keep something from passing through
		B	an area in a city enclosed by four streets
6	She bumped into a tree when she fell off her scooter.	**A**	struck against
		B	moved along in jerks and bounces
7	A part of the puzzle is missing.	**A**	a role in a play
		B	a piece of a whole thing
8	Did you see that butterfly land on the sunflower?	**A**	a part of the Earth's surface
		B	come to rest
9	The pitcher sat on a bench during the game.	**A**	a container for a liquid
		B	a member of a ball team

More Than One Meaning
Set 2

EMC 2723
©2004 by Evan-Moor Corp.

More Than One Meaning
Set 2

EMC 2723
©2004 by Evan-Moor Corp.

More Than One Meaning
Set 2

EMC 2723
©2004 by Evan-Moor Corp.

More Than One Meaning
Set 2

EMC 2723
©2004 by Evan-Moor Corp.

More Than One Meaning
Set 2

EMC 2723
©2004 by Evan-Moor Corp.

More Than One Meaning
Set 2

EMC 2723
©2004 by Evan-Moor Corp.

More Than One Meaning
Set 2

EMC 2723
©2004 by Evan-Moor Corp.

More Than One Meaning
Set 2

EMC 2723
©2004 by Evan-Moor Corp.

More Than One Meaning
Set 2

EMC 2723
©2004 by Evan-Moor Corp.

Answer Key

Page 5 Super Sentence Sort

Order of answers will vary.

Who?
Some children
My pet dog
A green parrot
A terrible dinosaur
That lazy giant
Ten acrobats

Did What?
nibbled fruit
vanished
splashed in the water
hid
fell asleep
did tricks

Where?
in the treetops
in a dark cave
in the backyard
under an old log
in a circus tent
behind the castle

When?
a moment ago
long ago
all afternoon
at 6:00
late one night
for many days

Bonus: Answers will vary.

Page 17 How Is It Spelled?

Order of words will vary. Circled vowels
indicate bonus answers.

Set 1	Set 2
Long a	**Long a**
play	weigh
train	face
eight	faint
rein	spray
April	they
take	nail
Long e	**Long e**
me	beam
happy	bumpy
sweet	many
eat	tweed
funny	grease
bead	bleach
Long i	**Long i**
pie	tribe
I	fire
cry	bright
five	tie
light	eye
my	fry
Long o	**Long o**
go	hose
throw	loan
toe	groan
joke	hoe
float	phone
those	woke
Long u	**Long u**
cute	mule
human	cue
menu	fuse
uniform	fume
cube	flute
bugle	truth

Page 29 Real or Make-Believe?

1. real	10. real
2. make-believe	11. make-believe
3. make-believe	12. real
4. real	13. make-believe
5. real	14. make-believe
6. make-believe	15. real
7. real	16. make-believe
8. make-believe	17. real
9. make-believe	18. real

Bonus: Answers will vary.

Page 41 Alphabetical Order

Set 1

1. Amy baked cookies.
2. George hid Jake's kite.
3. Even foxes get hungry.
4. Lilies make nice outdoor plants.
5. Kim likes making noise outside.
6. Claire drew eight fancy goldfish.

Set 2

1. My parka won't zip.
2. Bobby grew orange yams.
3. I like playing the xylophone.
4. Don feeds giraffes in the zoo.
5. Sam squirted Susan's sweater.
6. When will William wrestle Wyatt?

Bonus: Answers will vary.

Page 53 Fairy–Tale Riddles

Set 1

1. fairy godmother
2. giant
3. wolf
4. Henny Penny
5. harp
6. prince
7. Turkey Lurkey
8. woodsman
9. Foxy Loxy
10. Jack
11. Cinderella
12. Red Riding Hood

Set 2

1. fisherman
2. elves
3. frog prince
4. fisherman's wife
5. king
6. shoemaker
7. Hansel
8. shoemaker's wife
9. Gretel
10. princess
11. magic fish
12. witch

Bonus: Answers will vary.

Page 71 Draw and Write

Students' writing will vary.

Page 91 Antonyms

Set 1	Set 2
ask–tell	difficult–easy
buy–sell	finish–start
pull–push	child–adult
dark–light	morning–evening
new–old	follow–lead
hard–soft	false–true
now–then	break–repair
before–after	many–few

Bonus: Answers will vary.

Page 105 Synonyms

Set 1	Set 2
begin–start	hard–difficult
shout–yell	ask–question
part–piece	find–locate
gift–present	fragile–delicate
make–build	brave–daring
happy–glad	allow–permit
go–leave	all–whole
fast–quick	buy–purchase

Bonus: Answer will vary.

Literacy Centers—Take It to Your Seat • EMC 2723 • ©2004 by Evan-Moor Corp.

Page 119 As Busy as a Bee!

1. as busy as a bee
2. as hungry as a bear
3. as quiet as a mouse
4. as light as a feather
5. as flat as a pancake
6. chattered like a monkey
7. as quick as a wink
8. as hard as a rock
9. sparkled like diamonds
10. walks like an elephant

Bonus: Answers will vary.

Page 129 Top Ten

Student lists 10 responses related to the Top Ten topic.

Bonus: Students ask 10 classmates to put a check mark next to their favorite answer from the top ten list.

Page 139 It's in the Mail

1. Mother
2. Maggie
3. Astronaut Bill
4. George
5. Cowboy Bob
6. Aunt Suzie
7. Tanisha
8. Ronnie
9. Grandma and Grandpa

Bonus: Answers will vary.

Page 153 They Sound the Same

Set 1

new–knew	son–sun
5 6	10 8

beat–beet	too–two
1 12	9 4

ant–aunt	blue–blew
3 7	11 2

Set 2

dough–doe	flour–flower
1 8	9 7

hole–whole	bored–board
5 10	2 11

sent–scent	our–hour
6 4	3 12

Bonus: Answers will vary.

Page 165 More Than One

Add **s**
chairs
ships

Word ends in **s**, **sh**, **ch**, **x**, or **z**—Add **es**
foxes
benches

Word ends in consonant followed by **y**—Change **y** to **i** and add **es**
cities
berries

Word ends in vowel followed by **y**—Add **s**
monkeys
boys

Word ends in **f**—Change **f** to **v** and add **es**
loaves
calves

Irregular plurals
mice
oxen

Page 179 More Than One Meaning

Set 1	Set 2
1. B	1. B
2. A	2. B
3. A	3. A
4. B	4. B
5. A	5. B
6. A	6. A
7. B	7. B
8. A	8. B
9. B	9. B